Climbing Mt. Fuji

A COMPLETE GUIDEBOOK

FOURTH EDITION

BY RICHARD REAY

AN OFFICIAL MT. FUJI GUIDE

B O U K E N
INTERNATIONAL PUBLISHING

Climbing Mt. Fuji

First Printing, 2017

Editor: Mary Elizabeth Duff

All Photographs by the author unless otherwise noted

ISBN: 978-0-9921623-5-1 (Paperback)
ISBN: 978-0-9921623-1-3 (EBook)

Fourth Edition

Printed in the USA

Bouken International Publishing
Victoria B.C. Canada

For rights information and bulk book orders, please contact Bouken.International@gmail.com

In Memory of Midori Suzuki

Midori a long-time Mt. Fuji guide and good friend was one of the kindest people I've ever had the pleasure to meet. On July 13th, 2019, after returning from a Mt. Fuji climb, Midori passed away from heart failure while napping at the 5th station.

Midori's unexpected passing was a shock to the Mt. Fuji community. Midori spent her last moments on Mt. Fuji, which she loved, and where she had so many friends. Midori spent the winters traveling the world visiting mountain guides and friends in other counties.

"She loved the Children of Nepal
And the Mountains they Lived In"

REVIEWS

Well worth it! This is a "must read" for anyone who wishes to be successful in climbing Mt. Fuji. Don't be fooled by the apparent simplicity of the mountain - it is a tough and grueling climb and Richard knows all there is to know about it.

The book is a comprehensive and easy to read recipe for what it takes physically and psychologically to get to the summit of this amazing but unpredictable mountain. The author covers all facets of preparation, equipment, training and most importantly, altitude.I was very fortunate to have Richard as our guide when a group of us attempted to climb Mt. Fuji early in July 2014. This was apparently the first weekend that the mountain was "open" and there were literally, thousands of people on the mountain.

This, together with the rain and cold on day one, was not the greatest of environments, but having read the book, none of it was a surprise and most of us were well prepared. Richard - as well as being knowledgeable and obviously well respected by the local people, was also genuinely concerned and caring of the well-being of the group. He set a slow and steady pace and constantly made sure that everyone was ok. All 19 of us made it to the summit. Having successfully completed past climbs to Kilimanjaro, Machu Picchu and Everest Base Camp, it was easy to underestimate Mt. Fuji. My advice to anyone who wants to climb this mountain is to read the book, it is time and money well spent and if you're really fortunate, you'll have Richard to guide you to the top. By Dave Macedo - Published on Amazon.

Fantastic Mt Fuji Climb: Excellent book by a very experienced guide. I read this comprehensive book and then climbed Mt Fuji summit with Richard together with my husband and girlfriends. Such a wonderful experience. It's very important to understand the complexities and potential dangers before you take on such a climb. We did it off-season in June and would not attempt this without such a guide. Richard not only educated us on the best route to take but he also showed us how to walk so we maintained our energy level and we did not suffer physically after the climb. So beautiful and once in a life time experience made possible and very memorable by Richard and his guidebook. Thank you Richard! By Nicki E. Titze - Published on Amazon.

Great Guidebook: I would have liked better quality maps with contours and stuff. But apart from this it's a great guidebook for climbing preparation. The author is also a Fuji guide and if you go to MyTokyoGuide.com you can book him direct for the climb. So, my copy is signed by the author!! Reading it back after making the ascent, it's possible to reflect on how accurate Richard has been in his writing and his climb preparation advice is all good. By anonymous - Published on Amazon.

PREFACE

WHY I WROTE THIS GUIDEBOOK

This guidebook is for all those people I have seen curled up sleeping on the rocks near the summit, too tired and too cold to climb any further. And for all those I have seen shivering, soaked to the skin in the freezing rain outside the mountain huts without adequate rain gear, looking enviously at the warm people inside. Likewise for all those people I have seen sluggishly limp down the descending trails in obvious pain.

There are far too many articles, blogs and even books written about climbing Mt. Fuji by individuals who have only climbed the mountain once or twice and consider themselves experts.

I have worked as a professional Mt. Fuji mountain guide since 2008 and have climbed Mt. Fuji over 350 times in all types of conditions. As one of the few non-Japanese guides on the mountain my job has allowed me to guide guests from all over the world; trek all four-summit routes; and complete countless one-day, two-day and numerous pilgrim climbs from the base of Mt. Fuji.

A highlight for me as a professional Mt. Fuji Guide occurred when I appeared in a Japanese television segment called, Japan's 100 Most Famous Mountains as a professional Mt. Fuji Guide on Japan's National Broadcasting Channel (NHK).

I have seen my fair share of mishaps on Mt. Fuji. A great number of these could have been easily prevented with a little pre-climb planning.

This guidebook provides accurate reliable information because it was written by a real Mt. Fuji guide who has years of climbing experience and every imaginable type of Mt. Fuji climb under his belt.

More and more people are now interested in climbing Mt. Fuji. Those who contemplate climbing Mt. Fuji search for practical information to plan their climb. This guidebook provides that trustworthy reference to give climbers the best opportunity to succeed.

As a professional Mt. Fuji guide, it is my privilege to share my experience and knowledge, including my qualified advice along with my personal recommendations that I commonly reserve for clients with all those who have set their hearts on climbing this majestic mountain.

INTRODUCTION

The main reason for publishing the original Climbing Mt. Fuji Guidebook was to fill a gap identified by my clients. At that time many complained of the lack of available English information about climbing Mt. Fuji.

The goal was to not only provide practical information about climbing Mt. Fuji but also to introduce some of the cultural rituals associated with climbing historic Mt. Fuji.

To climb sacred Mt. Fuji in the footsteps of historic pilgrims is to bond with a faith of great purity and devotion that is unique to Mt. Fuji. Due to the unparalleled beauty and near perfect symmetrical cone shape, Mt. Fuji is often selected as the theme of paintings, poems and literature. It made the World Heritage list due to the culture significance of the mountain.

Climbing Mt. Fuji is more than just a hiking experience. It is a unique cultural experience with its own set of unspoken customs that can be easily missed or stomped on unknowingly if not careful.

The people working on Mt. Fuji during the climbing season are a tight community who respect these historical traditions. As one of the few non-Japanese Mt. Fuji guides creating and maintaining wholesome relationships with locals is key to being accepted into this close-knit society.

I still recall the first time I climbed Mt. Fuji. It was a sunny August day with two fit friends, using the popular Yoshida Route. (What could go wrong). Around the 8th station, we noticed some climbers were turning back using the ascending route. We asked one of the climbers what happened, and they explained that a propane tank at one of the summit mountain huts exploded. **Mt. Fuji Rule # 1: Expect the unexpected.**

Not to be denied, we continued on. Finally, reaching the Yoshida Route summit. we quickly spotted the scorched side of the mountain hut where the explosion occurred. The explosion must have frightened the other climbers, as there were absolutely no other climbers around. (which for August is extremely rare) as we continued to hike around the rim of the crater to the Kengamine Peak. This is the highest summit of Mt. Fuji. Upon approaching the peak, we spotted the only other climbers on the entire summit: two young Japanese men in clean stylish black and white tuxedos making cocktail drinks. (Mt. Fuji Rule # 1). A site you may envision at a stylish bar not the summit of Mt. Fuji. These two young men had cocktail shakers, several types of alcohol canteens and seemed to be in the middle of creating a beverage.

When they finally noticed, us standing in front of them amazed at the sight, one of them asked in Japanese, **"Would you like something to drink?"**.

That was my first taste of Mt. Fuji and every climb since has been unique. Each one has been filled with new obstacles and for me, the mountain never loses its magic even after four hundred climbs.

TABLE OF CONTENTS

Table of Contents

LIST OF MAPS

Table of Contents

LIST OF PICTURES

Climbing Mt. Fuji

CHAPTER ONE

MT. FUJI

Mt. Fuji

Majestic Mt. Fuji is the most renowned symbol of Japan and the highest mountain in the country standing at 3,776 meters or 12,388 feet. Because of its unparalleled beauty and near perfect symmetrical cone shape, Mt. Fuji is often selected as the theme of paintings, poems, and literature. To many Japanese it is also a spiritual source of worship and has been so for centuries.

Mt. Fuji is positioned on the border of two prefectures, Shizuoka on the southern side and Yamanashi on the northern side. It is the centerpiece of the Fuji-Hakone-Izu National Park and is surrounded by the five Fuji lakes, known as Fuji-goko in Japanese: Lake Kawaguchiko, Lake Yamanakako, Lake Saiko, Lake Motosuko, and Lake Shojiko.

On June 22, 2013, Mt. Fuji became a UNESCO World Heritage Site. It made the world heritage site list because of its cultural significance.

THE SACRED MOUNTAIN

After climbing Mt. Fuji many believe Fuji is Japanese for Stairmaster. In actuality, no one knows for sure where the real name came from. There are a number of theories about the origin of Mt. Fuji's name. One theory suggests it came from the Japanese Ainu aboriginal language meaning "fire mountain," while another says the name originated from the two Chinese characters 不尽 (not + exhaust) meaning "never-ending or "inexhaustible". However, it's clear that since ancient times Mt. Fuji has been considered a sacred mountain and even today it's used for various religious ceremonies.

Numerous Shinto shrines and Buddhist temples inhabit the mountain. Mt. Fuji is home to the Shinto Sengen Shrine, which has a long history of dedication to the official goddess of Mt. Fuji. The main Fujisan Hongu Sengen Taisha Shrine is located within the town of Fujinomiya near the base of Mt. Fuji. There are two branches of the Sengen Shrine located on the summit of Mt. Fuji. The Sengen Taisha Okumiya Shrine is located at the end of the Fujinomiya Trail and the Kusushi Shrine is located at the end of the Yoshida and Subashiri Trails. In fact, the entire top area of Mt. Fuji from the 8th station upwards is considered the precinct of the Sengen Taisha Okumiya Shrine, managed by the Fujisan Hongu Sengen Shrine. Every summer there are twenty wedding ceremonies held on the summit of Mt. Fuji at these two Shinto shrines.

The mountain was considered such a holy sanctuary that the act of climbing Mt. Fuji became a customary show of devotion for those wishing for happiness, health, and prosperity for their families.

Prior to the early nineteenth century females and non-Japanese were strictly forbidden to climb the sacred mountain. This changed in 1832 when Ms. Tatsu Takayama dressed up like a man and climbed Mt. Fuji: becoming the first female to reach the summit. Later, Sir Rutherford Alcock, the first British ambassador to Japan, (much to the distress of the government at the time) became the first non-Japanese to successfully climb Mt. Fuji. There is now a plaque honoring Sir Rutherford Alcock's accomplishment positioned at the trail's starting point at the Fujinomiya 5th Station.

Mt. Fuji is divided into ten stations or Go-mes as they are called in Japanese. At the base of the mountain is the 1st station (Gome) and so on until the summit, which is the 10th station (Gome). The stations are not equally spread out by distance or elevation. Just like the name Fuji, how the stations are spread out also remains a mystery. Reliable roads reach as far as all the 5th stations and there are parking lots at each one.

Sir Rutherford Alcock's Plaque

On a clear day, the distinctive silhouette of Mt. Fuji can be seen from as far as Tokyo: 100 kilometers away (62 miles). Until recently, most travelers visiting Japan simply enjoyed the beautiful scenery Mt. Fuji offered from the nearby lakes or aboard a passing bullet train on route to or from Kyoto.

Nowadays more and more travelers are adding a Mt. Fuji climb to their Japan "to do" list. In fact, numerous travelers now visit Japan just to climb Mt. Fuji making it one of the most climbed mountains in the world. Every year an estimated 300,000 people climb Mt. Fuji.

Until recently it was a common approximation that only one-fourth to one-third of all climbers climbing Mt. Fuji were believed to be non-Japanese, however with the vast increase in the number of visitors to Japan this has completely changed and this percentage skyrocketed to an estimated 50%. Of course, this percentage fluctuates from year to year due to certain events.

In 2019, the Rugby World Cup was hosted in Japan which attracted an unprecedented increase in the number of non-Japanese climbers.

On June 30th 2015, the Japan Meteorological Agency raised the volcano alert for Owakudani Park (Mt. Hakone) a popular tourism destination area in Hakone located within the Fuji-Hakone-Izu National Park to level 3 (do not approach the volcano).

Overall these events that increased the number of foreign climbers and reduced the number of local climbers has had an important positive impact for non-Japanese climbers. Until now many mountain hut owners, travel agents and Mt. Fuji associated venders that exclusively cratered too and relied on Japanese climbers for income; were suddenly forced to reconsider their business strategies and offer more global services.

Note about the Coronavirus: Due to the COVID-19 outbreak that started in early 2020, government officials announced that the 2020 Mt. Fuji climbing season will be cancelled. This is the first time since record-keeping started that Mt. Fuji did not open its trails. Both prefectures plan to carry out trail repairs for the opening of the 2021 climbing season.

CLIMBING FEE

In 2014, the prefectural governments surrounding Mt. Fuji introduced a ¥1,000 per person voluntary climbing fee. The fee was established to help with the increased environmental impact new climbers have on the mountain, including constructing new lavatories, expanding the number of first-aid centers and maintaining the exisiting facilities. Following final approval, the optional climbing fee is set to become a compulsory climbing fee starting from the summer of 2022.

The fee is collected on all four climbing routes. A toll collection booth is located at each route's fifth station. The Yoshida Route's collection booth was opened 24 hours a day from July 1st to September 10th. Collection booths on the three Shizuoka prefecture routes were open from 9:00am to 6:00pm from July 10th to September 10th.

In addition to the climbing fee the local governments also extended the period that private vehicles were restricted from accessing the 5th stations, allowing only buses, taxis and authorized vehicles access during peak summer periods.

While the overall number of foreign hikers climbing Mt. Fuji substantially increased, the actual number of Japanese hikers climbing during the official climbing season decreased, as many Japanese seemed to prefer to climb in the off-season to avoid these new restrictions.

VOLCANIC WARNINGS

Still considered an active volcano, Mt. Fuji is just one of 110 live volcanoes scattered throughout the seismically active country of Japan.

Strong earthquakes heighten the risk of volcanic eruptions in the region. This is exactly what happened the last time Mt. Fuji erupted some 300 years ago, on December 12th, 1707. Just 49 days after a violent earthquake of a magnitude 8.6 hit southern Japan, Mt. Fuji erupted spewing ash and smoke that could be seen as far away as Edo (Tokyo). This was when the enormous Hoei Crater on the Shizuoka Prefecture side of the mountain was created. (Edo is the previous name of Tokyo before 1868.)

More recently, on September 27th, 2014 Mt. Ontake, Japan's second highest volcano after Mt. Fuji, erupted without warning around midday, spewing ash, volcanic rocks and steam into the sky. Sadly, the explosion killed 63 hikers in the country's deadliest volcanic eruption in almost 90 years.

Mt. Ontake, located on the borders of Nagano and Gifu Prefecture, is around 200 kilometers (125 mi) west of Tokyo and approximately 100 kilometers (62 mi) from Mt. Fuji. Mt. Ontake volcanic warning was only at level one before it erupted, which is the lowest on the five-point risk scale and the current level of Mt. Fuji. Alert Level 1 is considered normal with no mountain restrictions. (See Volcanic Alert Scale on the next page.)

VOLCANIC ALERT SCALE

Volcanic Alert Level 1 = Normal
Volcanic Alert Level 2 = Do Not Approach Crater
Volcanic Alert Level 3 = Do Not Approach Volcano
Volcanic Alert Level 4 = Prepare to Evacuate
Volcanic Alert Level 5 = Evacuate

For the latest updates on volcanic warnings and weather advisories please check the Japan Meteorological Agency website. The site is available in English and displays the latest warnings of all types of weather and natural disasters, including; Eruption Notices, Earthquakes, Typhoons, Tsunami, Volcanic Warnings, as well as daily weather forecasts. As changes to the forecast and local conditions are continuously changing, a visit to this site is highly recommended when planning your Mt. Fuji climb and before starting your climb (www.jma.go.jp/en/warn/).

Note: If there were any large earthquakes in the area around Mt. Fuji or if the volcanic alert level of Mt. Fuji changes, it would be wise to postpone your Mt. Fuji climb.

Stars from Mt. Fuji - by Shunsuke Mizumoto

CHAPTER TWO

THE CLIMB

To climb sacred Mt. Fuji in the footsteps of historic pilgrims is to bond with a faith of great purity and devotion that is unique to Mt. Fuji. To climb Mt. Fuji - to be literally above the clouds looking down on the landscape and to witness a breathtaking sunrise can be the experience of a lifetime; however, do not underestimate the climb. Mt. Fuji is characterized by severe elevation gains, rapidly changing weather and steep inclines. The climb is unlike any high-altitude quest one will ever attempt. Do not believe the blogs and others who say, "Climbing Mt. Fuji is easy." While it is true under ideal conditions that some people have climbed Mt. Fuji in sneakers, jeans, and a sweatshirt, there are still many more who have attempted the climb using similar inadequate provisions and were miserably unsuccessful. Many people ascending Mt. Fuji for the first time underestimate the climb in three key areas.

First, they miscalculate the total time it takes to climb Mt. Fuji. Typically, it takes between six to seven hours to climb up the mountain and another three to four hours to descend. This is if you are leaving from the 5th station and then only taking the most popular Yoshida Route.

Secondly, the weather is easily misjudged. Extreme changes can occur despite weather forecasts. The weather on Mt. Fuji can never be accurately predicted. Unexpected rainstorms, thunderstorms, and heavy windstorms are common and hikers must be suitably prepared with the proper equipment.

Thirdly, many underestimated the elevation gain, which is approximately 1,500 meters or 4,900 feet from the 5th station on the Yoshida Route to the summit. This rapid ascent tests the limits of your physical and mental fitness. The air thins out as the elevation rises; thus, walking becomes difficult.

Overall, about 90% of the clients I have guided (both in and out of season) have reached the summit of Mt. Fuji; the other 10% were unable to reach the summit due to physical limitations or some type of altitude sickness. This percentage excludes those participants unable to reach the summit due to unanticipated extreme weather conditions.

Regardless of age, with proper gear and preparation, reaching the peak of Mt. Fuji is possible and extremely gratifying. As you stare down at the world below, the huge sense of accomplishment can be overpowering. And when you realize just how high you have climbed, it is truly a satisfying and memorable experience. It's hard to put it in to words, but sometimes when you watch the sunrise from the summit on a clear morning – it is a spiritual experience.

"In all of my many adventures in life, climbing Mt. Fuji ranks far above anything else I have ever experienced. If you have ever considered making this trip, I can say, without question you should."

~ Matt Horton - First Time Mt. Fuji Climber.

SHOULD YOU CLIMB MT. FUJI?

Anyone who climbs Mt. Fuji is personally responsible for his or her own safety. Thus, being in good physical shape and well prepared for the challenge is key. The more prepared you are for the climb the more gratifying your climbing adventure will be.

However, there is one type of person (throughout my years as a guide) who did not particularly enjoy hiking Mt. Fuji and would have appreciated anything else but climbing the mountain. These individuals are not there by choice. Instead they are there because their friends, family, or loved ones made the arrangements. For example, the boyfriend of the super lively girl that wants to try everything, or a group of old school friends that decides to try the climb.

My advice - if you are not interested in climbing Mt. Fuji then do not do it. Do not climb Mt. Fuji as a favor to a friend and do not let family or a significant other pressure you into the attempt. If you have no interest in climbing Mt. Fuji, then I recommend spending the night at a hotel or ryokan (Japanese style inn) at the base of the mountain. This is a perfectly acceptable alternative.

Even if someone is in great shape, climbing Mt. Fuji can at times be more mentally than physically challenging. So, if you are not fully committed to the climb, it is best to skip it and leave it to when you are committed.

The individuals who typically get the most out of climbing the mountain are well prepared, enjoy the outdoors, look forward to and enjoy the entire journey from start to finish – rather than just reaching the summit.

CHAPTER THREE

CLIMBING ROUTES

Once you have decided to climb this iconic mountain, the next choice is what route to take. There are four summit routes, each starting from one of the 5th stations. Three routes start in Shizuoka Prefecture and one begins in Yamanashi Prefecture. Each route has its pros and cons and offers its own distinctive scenery.

MAP #1: FOUR SUMMIT ROUTES

Fujinomiya Route

9.5th station
9th station
9th station
8th station
8.5th station
original 8th station
8th station
old 7th station
8th station
7.9th station
original
Yoshida Route
7.5th station
7th station
8th station
7th station
7.5th station
7th station
FUJI SUBARU LINE
5TH STATION
7th station
6th station
FUJINOMIYA
5TH STATION
6th station
7th station
6th station
KICKBACKS
Subashiri
Route
original
6th station
GREAT SAND RUN
7th station
SAND RUN
new 6th station
6th station
Gotemba
Route
SUBASHIRI
5TH STATION
GOTEMBA
5TH STATION

MAP #2: YOSHIDA ROUTE MAP

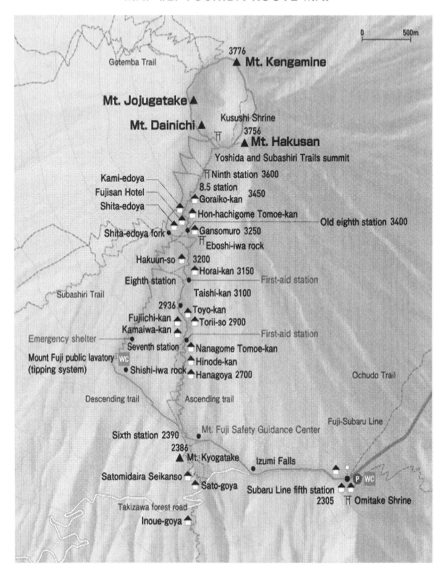

0   500m

Gotemba Trail

3776
▲ Mt. Kengamine

Mt. Jojugatake ▲

Mt. Dainichi ▲   Kusushi Shrine
      3756
      ▲ Mt. Hakusan

Yoshida and Subashiri Trails summit

Kami-edoya   Ninth station 3600
Fujisan Hotel   8.5 station
Shita-edoya   Goraiko-kan   3450
      Hon-hachigome Tomoe-kan
Shita-edoya fork ●   Gansomuro 3250   Old eighth station 3400
      Eboshi-iwa rock
Hakuun-so ▲   3200
      Horai-kan 3150
Eighth station ●   First-aid station
Subashiri Trail   Taishi-kan 3100
   2936 ● ▲ Toyo-kan
Fujiichi-kan ▲ ▲ Torii-so 2900
Kamaiwa-kan ▲
Emergency shelter ●   First-aid station
   Seventh station ▲ Nanagome Tomoe-kan
Mount Fuji public lavatory [WC]   ▲ Hinode-kan
(tipping system)   ● Shishi-iwa rock ▲ Hanagoya 2700   Ochudo Trail

Descending trail   Ascending trail

      Fuji-Subaru Line
      Mt. Fuji Safety Guidance Center
Sixth station 2390   ●
2386
      ▲ Mt. Kyogatake   Izumi Falls
Satomidaira Seikanso ▲
     ▲ Sato-goya   Subaru Line fifth station ▲ [P] [WC]
Takizawa forest road   2305   Omitake Shrine
Inoue-goya ▲

1. YOSHIDA ROUTE

ROUTE INFORMATION

- This is identified as the Yellow Trail.
- Only route that begins in the Yamanashi Prefecture.
- It is the most popular route (in-season).
- Total distance is 15.1 km or 9.6 mi.
- Average time up is six to seven hours (7.5 km, 4.1 mi).
- Average time down is four hours (7.6 km, 4.1 mi).
- Fuji Subaru Line 5th Sta is at 2,305 meters (7,562 ft.).
- The trail summit is at 3,720 meters (12,204 ft.) at the Kusushi Shrine.
- Separate ascending and descending trails.
- Access is by car (*see page 24), bus, or by train to Kawaguchiko Station and then a bus to the 5th station.

PROS

- There are many mountain huts.
- There are safety centers at the 7th and 8th stations.
- One guidance center at the 6th station.
- Many huts stay open into late September.
- Has the largest 5th station on the mountain with many restaurants and souvenir shops.
- Easy to access from Tokyo by bus, train or car.
- Sunrise side of the mountain.
- From this route climbers can enjoy views of Lake Yamanakako and Lake Kawaguchiko.

CONS

- Gets extremely crowded during peak periods.
- May have to wait in a line from the 9th station onwards to reach the summit.
- The descending trail has continuous switchbacks that get very tedious.
- Higher tendency for falling rocks (*see page 68)

The official name of the largest 5th station where the big tour buses stop (at the end of the Fuji-Subaru-Toll Line) is the "Fuji Subaru Line 5th Station". This is accessed by way of the Kawaguchiko Entrance, so some people refer to this as the Kawaguchiko 5th Station. The Yoshida Trailhead Route, which you enter from the bottom of the mountain, has its own separate smaller 5th station. The route from the Fuji Subaru Line 5th Station joins the Yoshida Route at the 6th station.

MAP #3: KAWAGUCHIKO ENTRANCE TRAIL

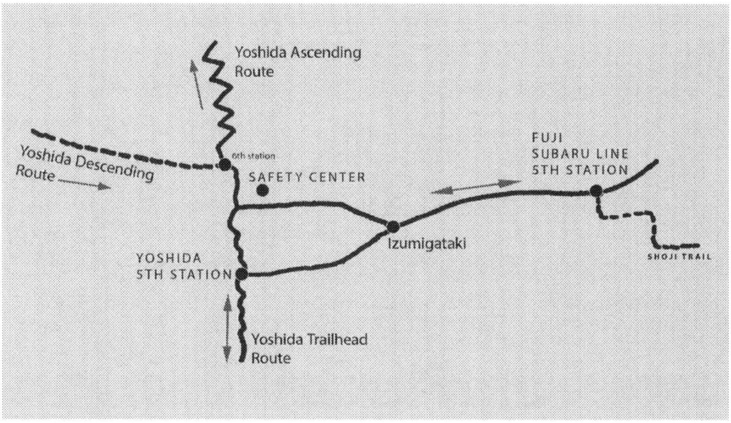

Yoshida Ascending Route

Yoshida Descending Route

6th station

SAFETY CENTER

FUJI SUBARU LINE 5TH STATION

Izumigataki

YOSHIDA 5TH STATION

SHOJI TRAIL

Yoshida Trailhead Route

The name of the short route from the Fuji Subaru Line 5th Station to the Yoshida Route 6th Station is referred to as the Kawaguchiko Entrance Route. On maps, the short Kawaguchiko Entrance Route is often combined with the yellow color code of the Yoshida Route, which causes some confusion.

This trail has 19 mountain huts, the most of any trail including three at the Fuji Subaru Line 5th Station and one at the Yoshida Trailhead 5th Station. The Fuji Subaru Line 5th Station is the largest of all the 5th stations with numerous restaurants and souvenir shops. If you forget any essential hiking gear it can be purchased at these shops at a premium. Ascending is on the sunrise side of the mountain, so hikers can enjoy the sunrise from the trail even if they do not reach the summit by sunrise.

ROUTE ACCESS

There are buses from Shinjuku direct to the Fuji Subaru Line 5th Station operated by the Fujikyu and Keio Bus Companies. Seat reservations are mandatory. Take note: they are not covered by the Japan Rail Pass or by the Fuji Hakone Pass.

Or you can also take the JR Chuo Main Line from Shinjuku to Kawaguchiko Station. (The Japan Rail Pass covers this JR train). Than take the bus from Kawaguchiko Station direct to the Fuji Subaru Line 5th Station.

MAP #4: FUJINOMIYA ROUTE MAP

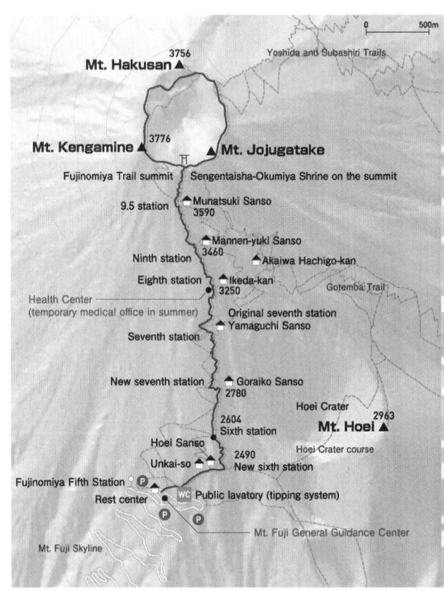

0 500m

3756
Mt. Hakusan ▲

Yoshida and Subashiri Trails

Mt. Kengamine ▲ 3776   ▲ **Mt. Jojugatake**

Fujinomiya Trail summit   Sengentaisha-Okumiya Shrine on the summit

9.5 station   ▲ Munatsuki Sanso
3590

▲ Mannen-yuki Sanso
Ninth station   3460
▲ Akaiwa Hachigo-kan

Eighth station   ▲ Ikeda-kan
3250   Gotemba Trail

Health Center
(temporary medical office in summer)   Original seventh station
▲ Yamaguchi Sanso
Seventh station

New seventh station   ▲ Goraiko Sanso
2780

Hoei Crater
2604   2963
Sixth station   **Mt. Hoei** ▲

Hoei Sanso
2490   Hoei Crater course
Unkai-so ▲ ▲   New sixth station

Fujinomiya Fifth Station P ▲
Rest center ● WC Public lavatory (tipping system)
P   P

Mt. Fuji General Guidance Center

Mt. Fuji Skyline

18

2. FUJINOMIYA ROUTE

ROUTE INFORMATION

- This is identified as the Blue Trail.
- It begins in Shizuoka Prefecture.
- This trail is the shortest route to the summit.
- Total distance is 8.5 km or 5.5 mi.
- Average time up is five hours (5 km, 3.1 mi).
- Average time down is three to four hours (5 km, 3.1 mi).
- The 5th station is at 2,400 meters (7,874 ft.).
- The trail summit is at 3,715 meters (12,188 ft.) at the Sengen Taisha Okumiya Shrine.
- The same trail is used for ascending and descending.
- Access by car (*see page 24) or train to Fujinomiya, Fuji, Shizuoka, Mishima Stations and then take a bus directly to Fujinomiya 5th Station.

PROS

- Has many mountain huts, one health center at the 8th station and a guidance center at the 5th station.
- All mountain huts higher than the 6th station are closed by the end of the first week in September.
- Quickest route to summit; popular in the off-season.
- From this route climbers can enjoy views of Suruga Bay and Izu Peninsula.
- Easy access to the Hoei Crater and Gotemba Route
- It's the closest trail to Mt. Fuji's highest Kengamine Peak (3,776 m, 12,388 ft.).

CONS

- This trail is on the south side of the mountain opposite to sunrise side of mountain.
- The ascending and descending routes are the same.
- Crowded during peak season, particularly in August.
- (*but not as crowded as the Yoshida route)

This is by far the shortest and most direct route to reach the summit and you can knock a good two hours off your ascending time and one to two hours off your descending time by choosing this route. There are nine mountain huts in total including the 5th station mountain hut and the summit mountain hut. The mountain hut staff are extremely friendly! As it is on the opposite side of the mountain to the sunrise, you will not be able to see the full sunrise before reaching the summit.

ROUTE ACCESS

To access the Fujinomiya Route take the bullet train from Tokyo Station to Mishima Station or Shin-Fuji Station (covered by Japan Rail Pass) and then take the climb bus (In-season only) directly from one of these stations to the Fujinomiya 5th Station.

MAP #5: MT. FUJI ACCESS MAP

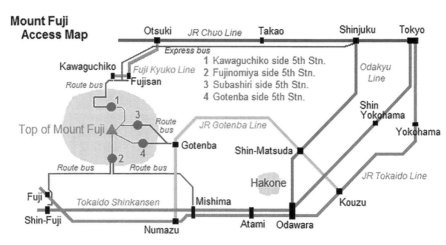

THE HOEI CRATER

Hoei Crater # 1 - Photograph by Shunsuke Mizumoto

The Hoei Crater shows the scars of the last Mt. Fuji eruption that occurred in 1707. The Hoei Crater, the largest crater on Mt. Fuji, is located on the southeast side near the Fujinomiya 6th Station. You can hike right into the base of the crater and to the peak of Mt. Hoei. The Hoei Crater can be accessed only from the Fujinomiya and Gotemba Routes and is routinely hiked throughout the year.

Generally, it is a safe hike, however, due to the wide-open position on that side of the mountain wind conditions are some of the strongest on Mt. Fuji. It is advisable to check the wind speed before climbing this trail.

MAP #6: GOTEMBA ROUTE MAP

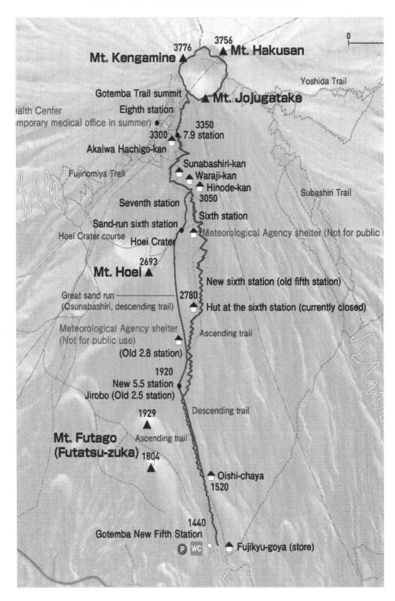

3776
Mt. Kengamine ▲

3756
▲ Mt. Hakusan

0

Yoshida Trail

Gotemba Trail summit
Eighth station
▲ Mt. Jojugatake

alth Center
mporary medical office in summer) ●
3300 ▲ ● 7.9 station
3350

Akaiwa Hachigo-kan

Fujinomiya Trail

Sunabashiri-kan
▲ Waraji-kan
▲ Hinode-kan
3050

Subashiri Trail

Seventh station

Sand-run sixth station
Hoei Crater course   Hoei Crater

Sixth station

Meteorological Agency shelter (Not for public

2693
Mt. Hoei ▲

Great sand run
(Osunabashiri, descending trail)

2780

New sixth station (old fifth station)

▲ Hut at the sixth station (currently closed)

Meteorological Agency shelter
(Not for public use)

Ascending trail

(Old 2.8 station)

1920
New 5.5 station ●
Jirobo (Old 2.5 station)

Descending trail

1929
▲

Mt. Futago   Ascending trail
(Futatsu-zuka) 1804
▲

▲ Oishi-chaya
1520

1440
Gotemba New Fifth Station
Ⓟ WC   ▲ Fujikyu-goya (store)

22

3. GOTEMBA ROUTE

ROUTE INFORMATION
- This is identified as the Green Trail.
- It begins in Shizuoka Prefecture.
- Longest route to summit.
- Total distance is 19.5 km or 12.2 mi.
- Average time up is eight to nine hours (11 km, 6.1 mi).
- Average time down is four to five hours (8.5 km, 5.5 mi).
- The 5th station is at 1,440 meters (4,724 ft.).
- The trail summit is at 3,715 meters (12,188 ft.) at the Sengen Taisha Okumiya Shrine.
- Separate ascending and descending trails.
- Access by car (*see page 24) or train to Gotemba Station then by bus to the 5th station.

PROS
- This is the most uninhabited trail so you meet few people on the trail.
- Great sand run on descending trail from the 7th station downward.
- Wonderful views of the Hoei Crater.
- You can hike the Hoei Crater; which is magnificent.
- Can crossover to the Fujinomiya Trail

CONS
- This is the longest trail.
- There are only a few mountain huts.
- This trail is on the opposite side of the mountain to the sunrise side.

This is by far the longest route to the summit and the least used trail. The Gotemba 5th Station is located at only 1440 meters (4,724 ft.). Currently, there are only four remaining mountain huts left on this trail. There are separate ascending and descending trails. The Gotemba Route is known for its great sand run, a straight path covered in soft lava gravel where you can literally run down a third of the mountain.

ROUTE ACCESS
To access the Gotemba Route take a train from Tokyo Station to Gotemba Station. The Japan Rail Pass covers this if you use the JR, or take the Odakyu Line from Shinjuku Station to Gotemba Station. Then take the bus from Gotemba Station direct to Gotemba 5th Station. The Japan Rail Pass does not cover the Odakyu Line.

MAP #5: MT. FUJI ACCESS MAP

Mount Fuji Access Map

Otsuki   JR Chuo Line   Takao   Shinjuku   Tokyo

Express bus
1 Kawaguchiko side 5th Stn.
2 Fujinomiya side 5th Stn.
3 Subashiri side 5th Stn.
4 Gotenba side 5th Stn.

Kawaguchiko
Fuji Kyuko Line
Route bus
Fujisan
Odakyu Line

Top of Mount Fuji
Route bus
JR Gotenba Line
Shin Yokohama
Yokohama

Gotenba
Shin-Matsuda

Route bus   Route bus
Hakone
JR Tokaido Line

Fuji
Tokaido Shinkansen
Mishima
Kouzu

Shin-Fuji
Numazu
Atami   Odawara

CRATER ROUTE TO KENGAMINE PEAK

Crater Trail - Photograph by Shunsuke Mizumoto

The last push to the highest point in Japan (Kengamine Peak) is characterized by an extremely steep gravel road on the rim of the crater to the final summit.

One of the best sunrise backdrops is from Mt. Fuji's Kengamine Peak. From here, while overlooking the summit crater, you can enjoy an amazing view of the sun rising from the horizon.

MAP #7: SUBASHIRI ROUTE MAP

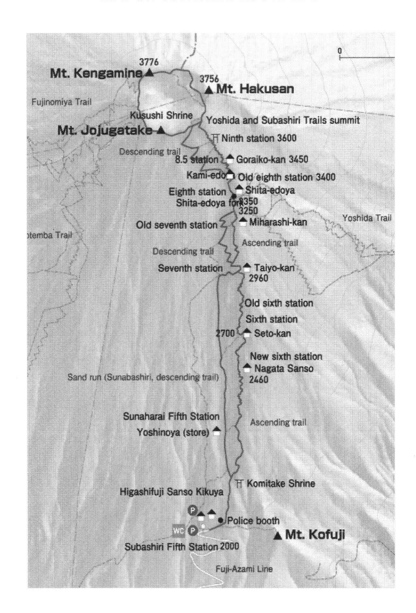

Mt. Kengamine ▲ 3776

3756 ▲ Mt. Hakusan

Fujinomiya Trail

Kusushi Shrine

Mt. Jojugatake ▲

Yoshida and Subashiri Trails summit

⛩ Ninth station 3600

Descending trail

8.5 Station ▲ Goraiko-kan 3450

Kami-edo ▲ Old eighth station 3400

Eighth station ▲ Shita-edoya

Shita-edoya for 3350

3250

Old seventh station ▲ Miharashi-kan

Yoshida Trail

otemba Trail

Ascending trail

Descending trail

Seventh station ▲ Taiyo-kan 2960

Old sixth station

Sixth station

2700 ▲ Seto-kan

New sixth station

▲ Nagata Sanso 2460

Sand run (Sunabashiri, descending trail)

Sunaharai Fifth Station

Yoshinoya (store) ▲

Ascending trail

⛩ Komitake Shrine

Higashifuji Sanso Kikuya

● Police booth

▲ Mt. Kofuji

Subashiri Fifth Station 2000

Fuji-Azami Line

4.SUBASHIRI ROUTE

ROUTE INFORMATION
- This is identified as the Red Trail.
- It begins in Shizuoka Prefecture.
- This is the heavily forested route.
- Total distance is 14 km or 8.1 mi.
- Average time up is seven to eight hours (7.8 km, 4.1 mi).
- Average time down is three to four hours (6.2 km, 3.1 mi).
- The 5th station is at 1,970 meters (6,463 ft.).
- The trail summit is at 3,720 meters (12,204 ft.) at the Kusushi Shrine.
- Separate ascending and descending trails.
- Access by car (*see page 24) or train to Gotemba or Shin-Matsuda Stations and then by bus to the 5th station.

PROS
- The trail winds through a lovely forest during the first hour or two of the hike.
- There is a sand section on the descending trail from the 7th station to where the forest area of the trail begins.
- This trail is on the sunrise side of the mountain.
- From this route climbers can enjoy views of Lake Yamanakako and Lake Kawaguchiko.

CONS
- This trail gets crowded from the 8th station onwards as it merges with the Yoshida Trail.
- Easiest trail to get lost on - dense forest area at night or in a thick fog.
- Higher tendency for falling rocks (*see page 68)

Subashiri 5th Station is at the 1,980-meter mark (6,463 ft.) and has separate ascending and descending trails from midway up the 5th station to the 7th station. There are 13 mountain huts in total including the ones at the 5th station and the summit. This is the only trail where you start by hiking through a dense forest area. Due to this dense forest and lack of climbers during off-peak dates, the Subashiri trail is easiest trail to get lost on.

ROUTE ACCESS

To access the Subashiri Route take a train from Tokyo to Gotemba, covered by Japan Rail Pass if you use the JR, or take the Odakyu Line from Shinjuku to Gotemba or Shin-Matsuda Stations, then take the bus at Gotemba or Shin-Matsuda Stations direct to the Subashiri 5th Station. The Japan Rail Pass does not cover the Odakyu Line.

* Note: Accesses to the 5th station's parking areas are closed to private vehicles during the peak-climbing season (each station sets their own closing dates). There are several parking lots at the base of the mountain where private vehicles can park and shuttle buses are provided to take hikers to the 5th stations during these times.

THE ORIGINAL PILGRIM ROUTES

There are also five original trails to climb Mt. Fuji from various spots at the foot of the mountain. Each trail merges with one of the four summit climbing routes at their various 5th stations. The use of these base trails has declined since vehicles and buses have been granted access to the 5th stations. Thus, they are not as well maintained and individuals' losing their way on these trails is a definite issue.

Depending on which base-trail you select anywhere from 10 km to 14 km (6 mi to 8 mi) will be added on to your Mt. Fuji climb. Therefore, additional time management planning is required. In spite of the extra time required, hiking from the base offers an alternative landscape of Mt. Fuji not seen when starting from the 5th stations. All but one of the original pilgrim routes starts from a Shinto Sengen Shrine near the base of the mountain. The Shoji Trail starts from Shojiko Lake.

1) THE ORIGINAL YOSHIDA ROUTE

The Yoshida Trail begins at the Kita Guchi Hongu Fuji Sengen Shrine at the base of the mountain, near the city of Fujiyoshida. According to the city: "This is where the pilgrims of over 800 years ago came to pray before they started their climb up the sacred mountain."

This trail is used for the city-sponsored Mt. Fuji Marathon at the end of July each year. It is by far the best maintained of all the original trails with several rest stops and washrooms available along the way (in the summer) to the 5th station. It connects with the summit route from the Kawaguchiko Entrance Trail, and the Subashiri Route at the 6th and 8th stations. If you are thinking of doing a pilgrim climb from the foot of Mt. Fuji this would be the best and safest trail to use.

2) THE MURAYAMA ROUTE

This route starts from the ancient Murayama Sengen Shrine, located near Fuji City. This is the oldest trail up Mt. Fuji, created 1000 years ago by the local villagers of Murayama. The trail was all but forgotten and abandoned after easier trails were opened in the early 1900s. However, in 2002, a Mt. Fuji club renewed the trail and it is now open to hikers again. The trail starts at 500 meters (1,640 ft.) above sea level and goes through the Omotefuji Green Campsite, 2nd station forest road and the Takabachi parking area before joining the Fujinomiya Trail at the 5th station.

3) THE SUYAMA ROUTE

Like the original Murayama Route, the Suyama Route had been neglected after easier trails were opened. The trail starts from the Suyama Sengen Shrine near Ashitakayama and is now a mixture of city streets and small trails before bordering the "Golf Park Bundy" golf course. Once you reach the Suyama Otainai Entrance, on the opposite side of the Mt. Fuji Skyline Highway, you know you are on the right path as the trail becomes clearer and better marked. From here you follow the path up the mountain until finally joining the Fujinomiya Trail at the 5th station.

4) THE SUBASHIRI ROUTE

Created some 800 years ago, the Subashiri Trail starts from the Niihashi Sengen Shrine near Gotemba Station and runs parallel to the Hakone Eura Highway before intersecting the east self-defense force training grounds and following the Fuji Azami Line Road up the mountain. The trail passes by the smaller peak of Mt. Kofuji (literally meaning small Fuji) before joining the Subashiri Trail at the 5th station. There is a cross trail to reach the Kofuji Peak of 1,979 meters or 6,492 feet that takes about 20 minutes from the Subashiri 5th Station.

5) THE SHOJI ROUTE

The Shoji Trail is the only one of the five original pilgrim trails not associated with a Sengen shrine. The trail starts from Lake Shoji-ko and intersects the Aokigahara Forest, also known as the sea of trees.

The Aokigahara Forest has the unfortunate distinction of being called a haunted forest. Since the novel 'Kuroi Jukai' by Seicho Matsumoto was published in 1960, in which the characters are focused on joint-suicide in the forest, the popularity of suicide in the forest among those determined to take their final walk has increased.

However contrary to popular belief, the Aokigahara Forest is a beautiful dense porous lava based forest with hundreds of unique tree moles and ice caves. The hiking trail has been revitalized in recent years, continues upward on a clear path until it crosses the Fuji Subaru Line Toll Road at the 3rd station-Jukaidai parking area and then finally intersects with the Fuji Subaru Line 5th Station.

THE CIRCLE ROUTES
THE CRATER TRAIL (OHACHI-MEGURI)

Hiking around the crater of Mt. Fuji is called Ohachi-meguri (in Japanese this means circling the basin). There are eight sacred peaks on Mt. Fuji's crater; the Ken-ga-mine Peak is the highest of the eight peaks (3,776m, 12,388 ft.). Unfortunately, as most people are usually exhausted by the time they reach the summit, the Crater Trail is often skipped which is really too bad as it is one of the most spectacular trails on the entire mountain. On a clear day, you have breathtaking 360-degree panoramic views from all edges of Mt. Fuji.

The Mt. Fuji crater is about 600 meters (1,968 ft.) in diameter and 200 meters (656 ft.) deep. The 4 km (2.8 mi) crater trail runs around the rim of the crater and it takes about 90 minutes to circle all eight of Mt. Fuji's summit peaks.

An unmanned weather station on Ken-ga-mine Peak, the highest of the eight summit peaks is a popular destination in the summer. In the morning, just after sunrise, many climbers line up in front of the marker next to the weather station to get their pictures taken, as this marker is recognized as the highest point in Japan. (See picture of Mt. Fuji's Kengamine Marker on page 106).

MAP #8: THE CRATER TRAIL (OHACHI-MEGURI)

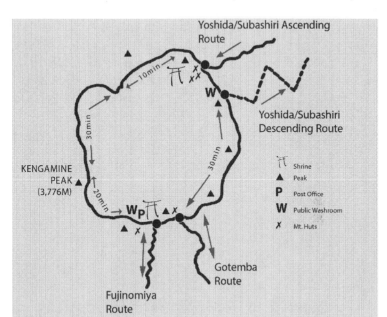

Note:
The crater loop is usually not included in the price of Group climbing tours, so if you join a tour and want to do the additional trek around the rim be prepared to pay an extra ¥500 to ¥1,000 per person depending on the size of the group.

THE OCHUUDO TRAIL

Formerly, the Ochuudo Trail circled the entire mountain near the 5th and 6th stations. Unfortunately, due to lack of use and landslides, this is no longer true. A few remaining sections of the original trail can still be found. The best maintained segment of the original trail in use today is a quaint 2.5 km (1.9 mi) hike starting from the Fuji Subaru Line 5th Station heading west. This short scenic trail parallels the Fuji Subaru-Line Toll Road and offers countless benches for resting and picture taking.

MAP #9: THE OCHUUDO TRAIL

OSAWA FAULT

OCHUUDO TRAIL

1hr

Oniwa

OCHUUDO TRAIL

1hr

FUJI SUBARU LINE 5TH STATION

OCHUUDO TRAIL

FUJI SUBARU LINE

SHOJI TRAILHEAD ROUTE

1hr

2hr

1hr

90 min

3rd station

JYUKAI DAI

34

THE PRINCE ROUTE

In 2008, the Crown Prince of Japan, Naruhito (now Emperor of Japan) successfully climbed the Fujinomiya side of Mt. Fuji. Rather than taking the ordinary Fujinomiya Route up Mt. Fuji, the Prince started from the Fujinomiya 5th Station and hiked up to the 6th station then turning right, cut through the Hoei Crater to join the Gotemba Route. After that he climbed up to the summit by means of the Gotemba Route. Once at the summit Prince Naruhito looped clockwise around the crater before descending the Gotemba Route finishing his climb at the Gotemba 5th Station. This route, which is also an enjoyable way to climb Mt. Fuji, is now appropriately called the Prince Route

MAP #10: THE PRINCE ROUTE

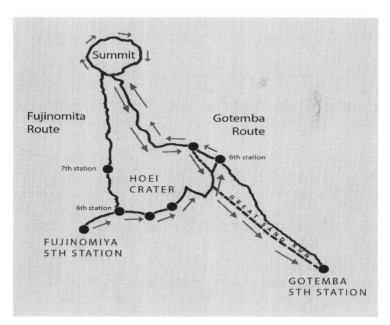

RECOMMENDED SUMMIT ROUTES

As each trail offers unique scenery, hiking separate trails for the ascending and descending routes is suggested and with four distinctive routes there are a total of sixteen possible route combinations to choose from. See my suggested route combinations based on the summer months below.

JULY & AUGUST: RECOMMENDED ROUTE

Ascending: Fujinomiya Trail
Descending: Gotemba Trail
+ Hoei Crater Trail back to Fujinomiya 5th Station

KEY ROUTE POINTS
- You get to the summit the fastest way.
- You avoid the overcrowded bottleneck on the Yoshida Route, specifically in August.
- Walk through the stunning Hoei Crater.

Description: Take the Fujinomiya Route from the Fujinomiya 5th Station up to the summit of the mountain. Stop along the way or stay the night to experience the friendly mountain hut staff on this side on the mountain. From the summit take the Gotemba Trail down, as this is the least crowded trail in August! When you reach the Kudari 6th Station, take the right-hand trail towards the Hoei Crater. This trail goes right down into the bottom of Hoei Crater. From the Hoei Crater bottom, there is a trail that goes up to join the Fujinomiya Trail 6th Station. Take this trail and return to the Fujinomiya 5th Station via the Fujinomiya descending route.

Hoei Crater # 2- Photograph by Shunsuke Mizumoto

SEPTEMBER: RECOMMENDED ROUTE

Ascending: Subashiri Trail (Yoshida Trail after 8th station)
Descending: Subashiri Trail

KEY ROUTE POINTS
Enjoy numerous mountain hut rest stops on the Yoshida ascending route from the 8th station onwards.
Avoid the dreary Yoshida switchback-descending trail.
Enjoy the Subashiri descending sand route
Enjoy Subashiri's charming 5th station and forest route.

Many mountain huts on the Subashiri and Yoshida Trails remain open until the end of September. Hiking these trails in early July or during the month of September is recommended as there are fewer hikers on the trail during these months.

Description: Start from the Subashiri 5th Station and take the Subashiri Route up unit the Shita Edoya 8th station Mountain Hut and cross-over right to the Yoshida Trail. Take Yoshida Trail to the summit. From the summit take the descending Yoshida/Subashiri Route, then take the Subashiri (descending) Trail at the 8th station. Do not miss the turn off just after the Shita Edoya Mountain Hut, as this is one common area that gives climbers enormous difficulties (refer to Tricky Trails in Chapter Six: Climbing Safety and Hazards). Enjoy the Subashiri Route forest trek and descending sand route, a much nicer alternative to the Yoshida descending switchbacks.

RECOMMENDED NON-SUMMIT TRAILS

Besides the four summit trails, there are hundreds of other smaller trails around Mt. Fuji. Beginners can hike many of these trails in the off-season as they are situated at a much lower altitude.

THE YOSHIDA PILGRIM ROUTE

The Yoshida Pilgrim Route starts from the Kita Guchi Hongu Shrine at the foot of Mt. Fuji and continues on to the Fuji Subaru Line 5th Station. This route takes from about four to five hours and is a very enjoyable and historical hike; beginners can do it.

Taking the traditional Pilgrim Route from the bottom allows hikers and climbers alike to enjoy the historical and cultural heritage along the path. This route is well maintained with several temporary washroom locations and resting spots. The Nakanochaya Teahouse is located at 1,100 meters or 3,608 feet, about 90 minutes along the route from the shrine.

MAP #11: THE YOSHIDA TRAILHEAD ROUTE

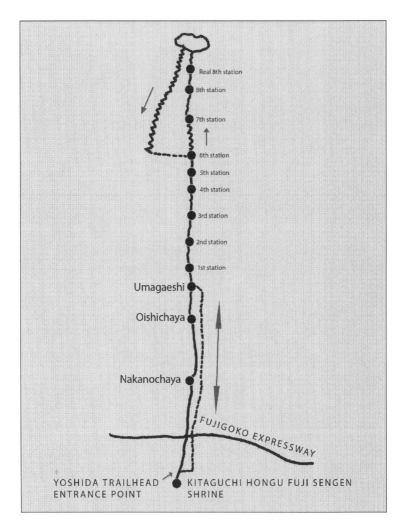

Real 8th station

8th station

7th station

6th station

5th station

4th station

3rd station

2nd station

1st station

Umagaeshi

Oishichaya

Nakanochaya

FUJIGOKO EXPRESSWAY

YOSHIDA TRAILHEAD
ENTRANCE POINT

KITAGUCHI HONGU FUJI SENGEN
SHRINE

40

GOTEMBA 5TH STA TO FUJINOMIYA 5TH STA ROUTE

Hiking from the Gotemba 5th Station at 1,440 meters (4,724 ft.) to the Fujinomiya 5th Station at 2,400 meters (7,874 ft.) and passing through the Hoei Crater is a very enjoyable hike with several different trail options. Doing a complete loop or starting and finishing from the Gotemba 5th Station is also possible as a day hike.

OPTION #1: GOTEMBA 5TH STATION TO FUJINOMIYA 5TH STATION THROUGH HOEI CRATER

Start from the Gotemba 5th Station, go up the normal Gotemba Route until you reach the Gotemba 6th Station. There, turn left down into the Hoei Crater until you reach the bottom of the crater, from here join the trail up to the Fujinomiya 6th Station. It takes about four to five hours and can be done by beginners.

OPTION #2: COMPLETE LOOP

Take the lower trail between the two Futatsuzuka hills to Fujinomiya 5th Station and return using the Hoei Crater Trail to Gotemba 6th Station and follow the sand run down to the Gotemba 5th Station. A complete loop will take about six to seven hours and takes the enjoyable Gotemba descending sand run, a straight path covered in loose lava gravel where you can literally run down the mountain.

MAP #12: GOTEMBA 5ᵀᴴ STA TO FUJINOMIYA 5ᵀᴴ STA

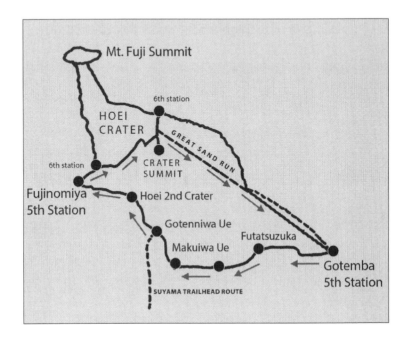

CHAPTER FOUR

MOUNTAIN HUTS

MT. FUJI MOUNTAIN HUTS

Mountain hut lodgings on Mt. Fuji are fairly simple, offering dormitory style bunk beds with blankets and sleeping bags. Do not expect hotel type conditions with separate rooms. Reservations are taken care of if you join a group or private tour.

Mt. Fuji Mountain Hut (Gansomuro)

Mt. Fuji Mountain Hut Staff (Hakuun-so)

However, if you plan your own climb you will have to make your own mountain hut reservation. There is a list of mountain huts, including contact information, provided at the end of this chapter. Due to the limited information about mountain huts available, many climbers do not consider the actual shelter itself when choosing where to stay. They simply select any hut located somewhere near the summit so they do not have far to climb the following day. However, choosing the right mountain hut can significantly add to the value of your Mt. Fuji climbing experience.

There are over 45 mountain huts on Mt. Fuji and each hut is individually operated. Each individual owner; sets their dates of operation, hires staff, creates their unique breakfast and dinner menus, sets the price, and decides on their own sleeping provisions. And just like all resort hotels everywhere, some are great places to stay and some are not so great. One might wonder, how great can the difference be? In actuality, the difference between the finest and nastiest mountain hut is incredible!

The lodging at the Toyo-kan on the Yoshida Route is one of the best on the mountain. It is professionally run, modern and clean. For dinner, the menu offers a delicious hamburger with miso soup and rice and their washrooms are extremely clean. From the washrooms, there is an unexpected superb view of the landscape below. I always make sure to stop for a washroom break here, even if I am not staying the night (price: ¥8,500~¥11,500 including two meals).

Hakuun-so Hut is another recommended place to stay. It is located on the Yoshida Route at 3,200 meters (10,498 ft.) altitude. The Hakuun-so Hut is clean, well organized and the resting space in front of the hut is the largest on the mountain. The resting space gives you heaps of room to stretch out and appreciate the sunset and the stars at night. The extremely friendly staff always greets you with a big smile to make you feel welcome. Dinner is curry and rice, topped with a hamburger (price: ¥8,500~ ¥11,500 including 2 meals).

If you are climbing the Fujinomiya Route, the best places to stay are the Munatsukisanso Hut at 3,590 meters (11,778 ft.) at the 9.5th station or the Mannen-Yukisanso Hut at 3,460 meters (11,351 ft.) at the 9th station.

Both huts are located at the higher 9th station, but climbing the extra distance to reach one of these is well worth the effort. The accommodation and meals they offer may not be extraordinary; however, the staff at both locations are so friendly you will be thankful you made the additional journey (price: for both mountain huts: ¥8,500 including two meals).

The Taiyo-kan at 2,960 meters (9,711 ft.) on the Subashiri Route remains open longer than any mountain hut on Mt. Fuji. (June 1 to October 15). So, if you are contemplating a 2-day off-season climb in October staying here is your only option.

For dinner, their set menu is rice, a hamburger and tonjiru (pork soup). Refills of rice and tonjiru (pork soup) are free. For breakfast they have grilled salmon, rice and miso soup, again refills of rice and miso soup are free.

On the other end of the mountain hut scale are the Fujisan Hotel at 3,400 meters (11,154 ft.) on the Yoshida Route and the Ikedakan at 3,250 meters (10,662 ft.) on the Fujinomiya Route. Staying at one of these two huts feels a lot like spending the night in a military camp, including the meals. After a night of following their strict commands and rules you will be so delighted to be released in the morning that you may forget you still have to climb to the summit. The Ikedakan Lodge on the Fujinomiya Route has the strictest timetable on the entire mountain. Arriving after 6:00 pm means no dinner for you even if paid for in advance.

LIST OF MOUNTAIN HUTS

YOSHIDA ROUTE: MOUNTAIN HUTS

Mountain Hut	Sta	Alti	Max	In-Season	Off-Season
Goraiko Kan	8.5th	3,450	140	0555-73-2179	0555-73-8815
Hon-Hachi-Tome Kan	8th	3,400	200	0555-73-1310	0555-24-6511
*Fujisan Hotel	8th	3,400	350	0555-22-0237	0555-24-6512
*Ganso Muro	8th	3,250	200	090-4549-3250	090-4549-3250
*Hakuun So	8th	3,200	300	0555-22-1322	0555-24-6514
Horai Kan	8th	3,150	150	0550-22-3498	0555-24-6515
Taishi Kan	8th	3,100	350	0555-24-1947	0555-22-6516
*Toyo Kan	7th	3,000	320	0555-22-6517	0555-24-1040
Torii So	7th	2,900	300	080-2347-5014	0555-84-2050
Fuji Ichi Kan	7th	2,800	120	080-1036-6691	080-1036-6691
Kawaiwa Kan	7th	2,790	150	080-1299-0223	0555-24-6520
Nana Gome Tomoe	7th	2,740	150	0555-24-6521	0555-73-1310
Hinode Kan	7th	2,720	150	0555-22-6522	0555-24-0396
Hana Goya	7th	2,700	150	090-7234-9955	0555-24-2208
Satomidaira Seikanso	6th	2,300	100	0555-24-6024	0555-24-6090
Sato Goya	5th	2,230	100	090-3133-2230	0555-23-1807

Climbing Mt. Fuji

FUJINOMIYA ROUTE: MOUNTAIN HUTS

Mountain Hut	Sta	Alti	Max	In-Season	Off-Season
Fujikan Hut	10th	3,770	150	090-3301-3512	0554-26-1519
*Munatsuki	9.5th	3,590	150	090-7300-2237	090-5855-8759
*Mannenyuki	9th	3,460	250	090-7025-2236	0544-27-2355
*Ikedakan	8th	3,250	250	090-2772-2235	0544-26-0512
Yamaguchisan-so	7th	3,010	180	090-7022-2234	0544-23-3938
Goraikosanso	7th	2,780	180	090-4083-2233	0544-26-3942
Hoeisanso	6th	2,493	80	090-7607-2232	0544-26-4887
Unkaiso	6th	2,493	80	090-2618-2231	0544-26-4533
5th Sta Rest House	5th	2,400	30	090-5002-2315	090-7618-2230

GOTEMBA ROUTE: MOUNTAIN HUTS

Mountain Hut	Sta	Alti	Max	In-Season	Off-Season
Akaiwa-Hachigokan	7.9th	3,350	150	090-3155-5061	0550-89-0703
Sunabashiri-kan	7.5th	3,090	150	090-3155-5061	0550-89-0703
Waraji-kan	7.4th	3,050	40	090-7301-5070	0550-89-0911
Oishi Chaya	5th	1,520	50	090-8955-5076	0550-89-2941

SUBASHIRI ROUTE: MOUNTAIN HUTS

Mountain Hut	Sta	Alti	Max	In-Season	Off-Season
Ogi-ya	10th	3,740	80	090-1563-3513	090-1563-3513
Yamaguchi-ya	10th	3,740	250	090-5858-3776	090-5858-3776
Goraiko Kan	8.5th	3,450	140	0555-73-8815	0555-73-8987
Kami Edoya (up)	8th	3,400	200	090-2770-3518	0550-75-3600
Shita Edoya (Down)	8th	3,350	250	090-2770-3517	0550-75-3600
Miharashi Kan	7th	3,250	120	090-1622-1048	0550-89-1048
*Taiyo Kan	7th	2,960	150	090-3158-6624	0550-75-4347
Seto Kan	6th	2,700	120	090-3302-4466	0550-89-0374
Osada Sanso (up)	6th	2,400	25	090-8324-6746	0550-89-3058
Yoshinoya (Down)	6th	2,400	Rest	090-7854-7954	0550-75-2019
Higashi-Fuji	5th	2,000	50	090-3254-5057	0550-75-2031
Kikuya	5th	2,000	70	090-8680-0686	0550-75-5868

* Mountain huts mentioned in this chapter.

RECOMMENDED MOUNTAIN HUTS

Yoshida Route: Gansomuro 8th Station
Yoshida Route: Hakuun so 8th Station
Fujinomiya Route: Mannenyuki sanso 9th Station
Fujinomiya Route: Yamaguchi sanso 7th Station
Gotemba Route: Akaiwa-Hachigoukan 7.9th Station
Subashiri Route: Taiyo Kan 7th Station

49

CHAPTER FIVE

EQUIPMENT

Having the proper gear greatly enhances the quality of your experience. The better equipped and the better quality the equipment is, the greater chance your excursion will be safe and comfortable. Quality gear is the best protection from the elements and provides a superior overall experience on your quest of Mt. Fuji.

The list below is divided into three categories:
- What to Bring
- Recommended to Bring
- What not to Bring

Hiking Equipment

WHAT TO BRING: BASIC EQUIPMENT

CLOTHING

Hiking Shoes: Comfortable and waterproof with thick soles. Stiff support to above the ankles is best.
Socks: Thick hiking socks (one quality pair is enough) made from synthetic fiber or wool. Must be able to absorb sweat.
Underclothing: Should be comfortable and loosely woven to provide ventilation – 100% polyester is an excellent lightweight synthetic – stays dry and cool.
Shirt: Comfortable, quick drying, polyester shirt + lightweight fleece.
Pants: Comfortable, stretchable, warm and light, quick dry with UPF 30+ (middle layer).
Rain Jacket and Pants: Water-resistant and windproof with a hood. Gore-Tex is preferred (outer layer).
Headgear: A breathable sun hat with large brim and UPF 30+ protection and a warm cap for the cold summit is recommended.
Gloves: Should protect climbers from the cold as well as the rocks.

OTHER NECESSITIES

Backpack: Must have capacity for at least 25 liters and a waterproof rain cover.
Backpack Rain Cover: Most backpacks are not waterproof.
Flashlight or Headlight: A light is mandatory even if you are not climbing during the night.
Sunscreen: SPF 50++ Sun Protection Factor. The sun's rays at higher altitudes have a much higher burning capacity than at sea level.

Medicated Lip Stick: Keep the lips moist to prevent dry chapped cracked lips.

Sunglasses: With UV protection, some bring ski goggles for protection against the sand and dust on the descending trip.

Trash Bags: For carrying your trash. Also good to keep valuables dry when it rains.

Water: Each person needs at least 1.5 to 2 liters. Water can also be bought at the mountain huts along the way.

> **Tip: Buy water from a mountain hut. Then refill your existing water bottle and return the empty plastic bottle back to the mountain hut from where you bought it; they accept all empty bottles they sell.**

Food: Climbing is a strenuous activity and has high-energy requirements. Bring high-energy snacks: nuts, chocolate, energy bars and trail mix. Mt. Fuji is not the place you should be dieting or the place you want to be counting calories. You need to be continuously feeding your furnace to provide the energy required for the climb. To climb Mt. Fuji takes the same number of calories as a full-length marathon. Consuming foods high in fats enables a sufficient calorie intake.

Money: Bring a minimum of ¥6,000 including ¥100 coins to cover all your toilet stops, bottles of water and to enjoy a noodle breakfast at the summit. If you are getting your walking stick stamped along the way, add another ¥3,000. If you are staying at a mountain hut, it will cost another ¥8,000 ~ ¥11,000 – depending on which hut you stay at.

RECOMMENDED TO BRING

Camera: To capture spectacular photos, particularly the sunrise (weather permitting).

Insurance Documentation: The purchase of traveler's insurance, which provides full medical and emergency evacuation coverage is recommended due to the risk involved.

Trekking Poles: Poles provide good stability and reduces stress on knees.

First Aid Kit: Basic materials to treat minor cuts and ailments especially if you climb without a guide.

Towel: A small terrycloth towel helps dry off sweat and clean the dust from your face.

Toiletries: Toothbrush, toothpaste, and sanitary wipes.

Mask or Face Cover: Covering your nose and mouth is very useful for the extremely sandy and dusty descending routes.

Ear Plugs and Eye Mask: If you would like to sleep on a two-day climb in August it is recommend you bring these, as the huts are extremely noisy during the night.

Sandals: Bring sandals to change into when you finish the climb.

Spates/Gators: Not absolutely compulsory for a Mt. Fuji climb, but they will keep your socks dry in the rain and keep rocks out of your shoes, especially on the descending sand trails.

Playing Cards: For two-day climbs, you may have up to eight hours to kill at the mountain hut with little to do, so bringing a deck of cards helps pass the time and may aid you in making new friends (UNO is a nice alternative).

WHAT NOT TO BRING

Drones: From all 5th Stations up to the summit, Mt. Fuji has implemented a strict no fly zone.

Cotton T-Shirts: Once wet from rain or perspiration they stay wet: keeping your body damp and cold.

Jeans or Jean Shorts: Denim material is just not meant for climbing; it does not stretch or breathe and becomes very hot in the sun and when it gets wet it stays wet.

Under Armour Shirts: These tight shirts that are meant to show off your muscles, may look cool in the gym, but on the mountain they are far too restrictive.

Aqua/Water Sports Shoes: Sometimes called water socks, or surf shoes (the ones with the individual toes). These are absolutely not intended for mountain climbing.

Sleeping Bags: All mountain huts provide blankets and or sleeping bags.

iPad: Bringing an iPhone is fine if it has a protective case; however, iPads or iPad Minis are too big and awkward and are easily broken on the mountain.

Credit Card: Cash is king on Japan and Credit Cards are generally not accepted on the mountain huts.

Running Shoes and Sneakers: Some people have successfully climbed Mt. Fuji in basic running shoes. The problem occurs when it rains. This type of shoe is not waterproof so after they get wet they tend to become waterlogged and keep your socks soggy and mushy. I have even seen people wearing plastic bags inside their running shoes, trying to keep their feet dry after their shoes and socks have become waterlogged. Buying or renting a pair of good quality hiking shoes is highly recommended.

POLES OR NO POLES

Most serious hikers and climbers know the benefits of using hiking poles. Nevertheless, first time Mt. Fuji climbers often ask, "Do I really need to use hiking poles?"

My answer is, "Climbing Mt. Fuji with hiking poles will significantly save you energy, increase your balance and stability and reduce the stress on your knee joints, ligaments and leg muscles."

I have climbed Mt. Fuji over two hundred times and I really noticed the difference the few times I forgot my hiking poles. Without poles, after the climb, I experienced more leg, knee and foot pain. I always use hiking poles to set a good example for my guests and I always encourage clients to use them, if there is a choice.

Alas, many people that climb Mt. Fuji treat it more as a sightseeing occasion rather than a serious climb. So, instead of hiking poles many people opted to buy an official Mt. Fuji walking stick.

WALKING STICKS

The exact same style wooden Mt. Fuji hiking stick has been around for ages. The sticks are the best selling souvenirs on the mountain. For many who climb Mt. Fuji this is a "must have" memento. The typical walking stick is sold everywhere, including the 7-11s and other convenient stores around the base of Mt. Fuji.

They cost between ¥800~ ¥1,200; depending on the size and what is attached to the end of the stick. Attachments vary; from a map of the mountain, to the Japanese flag, to nothing at all.

The best point about purchasing a walking stick is that each mountain hut has its own unique stamp. So, you can get a stamp burnt onto your wooden walking stick at every hut you visit, including the summit mountain huts. Stamps cost between ¥200~ ¥500 each. Then when your trip is over, you have a wooden walking stick covered with unique mountain hut stamps to remember your Mt. Fuji climb and to prove to your friends that you reached the summit.

Practically speaking, walking sticks are a little heavy and can be cumbersome on the steep rocky inclines, although they can assist with balance on the steep declining parts of the trail. Overall, walking sticks are not a substitute for hiking poles and if you want to climb Mt. Fuji in the safest and most efficient way possible, hiking poles are your best option.

HIKING EQUIPMENT: RENTING VS BUYING

If you do not have all the necessary climbing equipment, the decision to rent or buy is completely up to you. If you plan on hiking again in the future, it may be more economical to buy your own equipment.

Conversely, if Mt. Fuji is the only mountain you intend to climb or if you left your gear at home, it might be sensible to rent instead of buying.

There are several places to rent hiking gear in Japan, either in person or through the Internet. I recommend Yama Rent and Sangaku Doumei. Yama Rent is conveniently located in Shinjuku near Shinjuku Station and has several friendly English speaking staff on hand. Sagaku Doumei is a local shop located at the base of Mt. Fuji.

Yama Rent also has an English website (See Link below) with pictures of all the rental gear so you can get an idea of the items and brands available before you rent. Both companies off free delivery within Japan when you spend over ¥5,000.

The Japanese domestic delivery system is very efficient. Online rental shops can deliver equipment to your hotel or any address in Japan. It is best to reserve your equipment well in advance. The equipment will be delivered a couple of days before your climb. After your climb, simply put all the gear in the bag provided by the rental shop and drop the bag off at your hotel or the nearest convenient store along with the original delivery slip received with the equipment. The delivery company will return the gear to the rental company free of charge.

Rental gear available includes: hiking poles, headlamps, backpacks, rain pants, rain jackets, gloves, hiking shoes, crampons, icepicks, sun hats, and sunglasses.

Yama Rent: Yamarent.com/en
Sangaku Doumei: Sangaku-doumei.jp/

CHAPTER SIX

CLIMBING SAFETY & HAZARDS

Before climbing Mt. Fuji there is a great deal to consider: such as, gear, accommodation, transportation, routes and whether to hire a guide or join a group. Likewise, during the climb, hikers need to consider the problems that may occur.

ALTITUDE SICKNESS

Hikers, particularly first time hikers, need to be aware of a condition known as altitude sickness. Altitude sickness is the body's reaction to decreasing amounts of oxygen in the air.

At higher altitudes above 2,400 meters (7,900 ft.) the concentration of oxygen in the blood decreases. Ascending rapidly up the mountain causes altitude sickness, usually ascending faster than 500 meters (1,640 ft.) per day. A typical Mt. Fuji climb ascends approximately 1,300 meters (4,265 ft.) in two days. Jet lag, lack of sleep and cold temperatures can intensify the effects of altitude. In my experience, about one in ten Mt. Fuji climbers experience altitude sickness. It affects even the strongest and fittest people.

The best way to avoid altitude sickness is to give the body time to adapt to the changes in altitude. This practice of adjusting to higher elevations is called acclimatization. A slow, steady ascent up the mountain is the key method used to acclimate the body to altitude changes.

Thus, one of the basic vital jobs of a professional Mt. Fuji guide is setting the appropriate climbing pace. Having a professional guide set the relevant hiking pace is an effective way to avoid altitude sickness. When climbing on your own you are more likely to ascend too fast and experience altitude sickness symptoms (refer to the zombie shuffle section).

Other effective ways to prevent altitude sickness includes drinking plenty of water (see dehydration section), eating a lot of easily digestible high calorie foods and knowing how to breathe steadily.

Breathing – When climbing at higher altitudes many forget there is less oxygen and breathe normally. When they do this, their body does not get the right amount of oxygen which contributes to altitude sickness. Therefore, deliberately increasing breathing repetitions to supplement the additional oxygen needed for the climb is required (refer to the mountain breathing technique section in this chapter).

Food – Due to the lack of oxygen in the blood at high altitudes, the body does not fully use the nutrients in food. Extra fuel is required to meet energy needs of increased elevation. Red meats should be avoided, as they take a long time to digest at high altitudes, and although foods high in carbohydrates like pasta offer a quick energy source for high intensive training, other research suggest foods high in fats like chocolate and nuts are a better energy source at high altitudes.

Medicine – The final prevention method for altitude sickness is a medicine known as Diamox.

Diamox is a mild diuretic prescribed by doctors, it reduces the buildup of body fluids. I have never actually used Diamox during all my years of guiding, but some clients who used it to prevent altitude sickness swear by the benefits. Please consult with your physician before trying Diamox.

ALTITUDE SICKNESS TREATMENT

Altitude sickness hits everyone differently. Many experience mild symptoms similar to a hangover, or get a headache, suffer a loss of appetite, encounter nausea, light-headedness, or even a mild stomachache; however, they can still continue to climb. Then again, when the symptoms go from mild to severe the best treatment is to descend to a point where you start feeling better. These symptoms may lessen with sufficient rest and water intake.

The rule of thumb is: if you get to a point where you throw up and afterwards you still do not feel a whole lot better, then it is time to head down the mountain.

Some climbers throw up from altitude sickness and after eating and drinking feel much better and are able to continue. However, when someone throws up and refuses to drink or eat afterwards; trouble is imminent.

Altitude sickness can be very serious. If someone experiences severe symptoms that do not improve after resting at the same altitude, do not wait to descend: no matter what time of day or night it is. As soon as possible descend to a point where they start to feel better and seek medical attention if needed.

ZOMBIE SHUFFLE

In the hiking world, there is a technique known as the "rest step". It is used when ascending high altitude mountains. The step consists of pausing the rear leg when fully extended and locking the knee. This puts all body weight on the rear leg while at the same time resting the front leg. The technique, the conscious practice of delaying the next step, is used to conserve energy and ensures a safe, slow, steady rate of ascent.

As the technical rest step is difficult for first time climbers to grasp, there is another less technical and easy move to master. This move I developed to help slow guests hiking pace is called the "Zombie Shuffle".

The Zombie Shuffle is exactly what it sounds like; it is a term to describe how zombies walk or shuffle along. Now, I realize there are no real zombies; however, based on the zombie movies I have seen, zombies have a unique walk. It is slow, sluggish and energy conserving – perfect for climbing Mt. Fuji. Typically, their heads are down, their arms and bodies are relaxed and they walk extremely slowly. Zombies in fact would make great mountain climbers and I am sure if they climbed Mt. Fuji, none would experience altitude sickness.

I often ask guests, especially at the beginning, to take slow small shuffle steps instead of walking normally, relaxing their entire body and literally walking like a zombie. This way they slow their pace and save energy. Some guests probably thought I was an idiot and were annoyed at how slow the hiking pace was at the beginning of the climb; however, none complained when we made the summit on time and had a lot of energy to spare for the descent.

In addition to a slow hiking pace, if starting a climb at a 5th station (like most who climb Mt. Fuji do), you need to give yourself time to acclimate to that altitude before starting the climb. This is especially important for those hiking from the highest 5th station – the Fujinomiya 5th Station. Usually one hour is enough for your body to acclimate.

DEHYDRATION

While climbing Mt. Fuji it is very easy to get dehydrated. Dehydration occurs quicker at higher altitudes and thirst is not necessarily a good indicator of how much water is needed. Overdressed climbers perspiring excessively due to hot temperatures combined with inadequate fluid intake and the drier air of higher altitudes leads to excessive fluid loss. This rapid dryness can lead to fatigue, headaches, dizziness, chapped lips, and nausea.

It is important to remind yourself to keep continually drinking water and to maintain an electrolyte balance with sports drinks targeted specifically for this purpose. It is a good idea to start hydrating prior to the climb. Drink at least 500 ml of water before arriving at the 5th station and another 500 ml of water before starting to climb. Avoid caffeine and alcohol, as these can increase the likelihood of dehydration.

MOUNTAIN BREATHING TECHNIQUE

Climbing Mt. Fuji requires more than the normal amount of oxygen. So, normal breathing can hardly supply enough oxygen, especially at higher altitudes. The higher you climb, the less oxygen there is in the air and the harder the heart pumps to compensate for the lack of oxygen.

There is a mountain breathing technique known as "pressure breathing". To do this you put your lips together and forcefully breath out, pushing all the dead air from the bottom of the lungs out, similar to when you are blowing out a candle.

This is done quickly three times followed by a slow deep inhale that completely fills your lungs with new air. This breathing technique allows you to increase oxygen intake as well as slow your heart rate. I practice this technique with clients especially near the summit to help them to relax, catch their breath, and raise their oxygen level.

PORTABLE OXYGEN CANISTERS

The portable oxygen canister is another hot selling item on Mt. Fuji. It is sold all over the mountain and comes in both the large five-liter canister and the smaller ten-liter pocket canister. Many people use oxygen as a stopgap measure for altitude sickness and swear by the benefits, while others who use it cannot tell the difference.

Some climbers find it difficult to sleep at high altitudes, as normal breathing during sleep does not provide the necessary oxygen. While spending the night in a mountain hut, many find oxygen quite useful as it relaxes their labored breathing.

For reassurance, if you are climbing on your own, carrying a portable oxygen canister is always a good idea. I recommend the smaller pocket oxygen canister as it contains more oxygen, is smaller and easier to carry.

TRICKY TRAILS

Most routes have separate ascending and descending trails that intertwine with other trails on the mountain, so trails get complicated at times.

In particular, there is one common area that causes climbers enormous problems when taking the Yoshida and Subashiri Routes. From the summit the Yoshida and Subashiri descending routes are the same until climbers reach the 8th station. At the 8th station there is a junction, where one trail leads to the Yoshida 5th Station and the other trail leads to the Subashiri 5th Station.

Many climbers who take the Yoshida Route up the mountain mistakenly take the Subashiri Trail down. I chatted with an English Guidance Worker stationed at the Subashiri 5th Station and she said every day during the summer climbing season at least 2-3 people came down the wrong trail and sometimes-entire groups made this mistake. It was her job to explain to fatigued climbers they took the wrong trail and give them options for returning to the correct 5th station or Tokyo.

The public bus takes three to four hours to return from the starting point of the Subashiri Trail to the starting point of the Yoshida Trail and costs ¥4,000. By taxi, it takes only an hour depending on the traffic but cost between ¥25,000~ ¥30,000 for a one-way trip. This problem has caused hikers to miss their tour buses.

When descending from the summit at the 8th station (Shita Edoya Mountain Hut) junction point climbers returning to the Subashiri 5th Station take a right turn at the trail fork and climbers returning to the Yoshida 5th Station continue straight passing by the Shita Edoya Mountain Hut (please refer to map below).

MAP #13: 8TH STATION DESCENDING JUNCTION

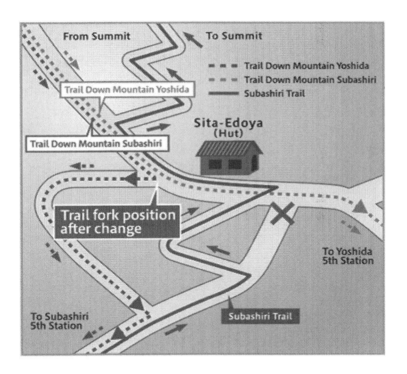

Diverging Point Signboard

TRAIL MARKERS

In an effort to clearly mark all major routes up Mt. Fuji, the Japanese Ministry of Environment (MOE) has created color-codes for all four major hiking routes.

COLOR CODES AND MARKER NUMBERS

Yoshida Route	Yellow	from Y-001 to Y-080
Subashiri Route	Red	from S-001 to S-080
Fujinomiya Route	Blue	from F-001 to F-056
Gotemba Route	Green	from G-001 to G-112

As well as developing color codes, the MOE has periodically marked each route with safety location markers. All the markers have a location number, which indicates where you are on the mountain, plus a SOS number (110) that when called puts you in direct contact with the local police.

For example: Marker S-022 indicates the Subashiri Trail at the 22-marker location. So, in the case of an emergency and you have a cell phone with reception, find the nearest marker, call 110 and let the authorities know the marker's number.

These markers can also be used as a rough estimate to gauge distances. Knowing the total number of markers on each route will help you estimate the distance to the summit. For example, there are only 56 markers on the Fujinomiya Route from F-001 to F-056, so when you reach the F-028 marker you are roughly half way there.

Warning Sign and Location Marker

FALLING ROCKS

Falling rocks and rockslides on Mt. Fuji have been a concern lately especially on the popular Yoshida trail located on the Yamanashi prefecture side of the mountain.

At the beginning of the 2019 Mt. Fuji climb season, a rockslide near the summit of the Yoshida trail apparently triggered by a typhoon caused a blockage of the trail and a delay in the opening of the Yoshida trail.

On the same Yoshida trail on Aug. 26th, 2019 a Russian woman in her 20's was climbing with a group, in the early morning when she was struck in the chest by a falling rock near the summit causing fatal injuries. After the incident, the Yoshida trail was closed again between the area before the 9th station and the summit until 6 p.m. on Aug. 26th.

In the early morning, climbers irritated by the long waits and logjams near the summit, sometimes try to dangerously pass others by climbing outside the trail boundaries in order to catch the sunrise from the summit. Climbing outside the trail borders is strictly forbidden as it can easily trigger a rockslide or single rocks to fall since the Yoshida trail from the 9th station upwards to the summit is surrounded by numerous unstable lava rocks.

Overall the number of reported rockslides is rare compared to the number of climbers that climb Mt. Fuji every year, however, all climbers should be aware that Mt. Fuji is structurally prone to falling rocks, especially if you are using the Yoshida route.

Rock Pile near Yoshida Route Summit

TYPHOONS

Typhoons are a regular and natural occurrence in Japan. Japan averages about 25 typhoons per year peaking in August and September. Typhoons may display heavy rainfall and winds of up to 200 km/h (124 mph). Western travelers may be familiar with similar storms that form over the Atlantic Ocean, which are known as hurricanes. Interestingly, typhoons are not given names in Japan as are their hurricane counterparts. Instead, they are given numbers: "typhoon # 1," "typhoon # 2," and so on.

Every climbing season 1~2 super typhoons cause some climbing dates to be cancelled. However, speaking from experience not all climbs need to be cancelled when a typhoon approaches. Generally, most typhoons in Japan have a predicable path when approaching from the south, hitting the southern Islands of Okinawa, Kyushu and Shikoku first and hardest, then the typhoon tends to weaken (downgrading to a tropical storm) as it gets closer to Mt. Fuji and Tokyo. When carefully observing the type and direction of a south approaching typhoon, most come at an angle and only last a half-day to a day when passing through. So, if you are doing a 2-day Mt. Fuji climb you may be able to time your summit to climb on the first or second day to avoid the typhoon. The weather before and after a typhoon is extremely clear and sunny and if you are able to time the summit the views are spectacular.

Nonetheless not all typhoons are the same and follow the same paths, last year (2019) a slow-moving super typhoon hit Tokyo directly causing 3 days of heavy rain and massive flooding, closing down all the highways and local trains and bullet train lines in the area.

If you are in Japan when a typhoon strikes, watch local news media for reports, including travel advisories. Flights, trains, and expressways may be closed during or after a typhoon, so you should plan your accommodations and activities accordingly. Before booking your late summer travel, check with your airline's cancellation policy.

Japan Meteorological Agency: This website provides the latest and most up-to-date information on typhoons in Japan. Bookmark it to get daily weather forecasts for your trip. It is also a reliable resource for earthquakes and tsunami advisories and warnings.

LIGHTNING

Thunder and lightning storms can materialize suddenly on Mt. Fuji. They are common in the late summer. As the bare volcanic terrain on Mt. Fuji leaves you totally exposed and lightning tends to hit the tallest object around, storms of these types can be extremely dangerous.

Up until now I have not been confronted with a real life-threatening situation on Mt. Fuji, however that changed early one morning on the summit when a rainstorm abruptly turned into a terrifying thunderstorm. A sudden loud crack of thunder caught all by surprise and scared the pants off everyone standing on the summit, but when a white flash of lightening smacked down just meters away from where I was standing seconds later, my heart nearly jumped out of my chest.

Lightning seeks the path of least resistance to the ground, which is often the shortest route. Standing on the summit while holding metal hiking poles is not a wise idea.

I have encountered severe lightning storms while climbing Mt. Fuji before, but usually from afar, this was the first time I experienced one on the summit.

Survival mode quickly kicked in. All the summit buildings were packed to capacity. Trying to sound calm I told the Australian couple I was guiding at the time, we must get off the mountain as soon as possible. I remember rushing past the post office without stopping, saying, "By the way there is the summit post office". After we reached a safer level we had a chuckle about our unique climbing experience. To this day, I can still easily recall the adrenaline rush I felt when the lightening hit.

If you are caught in a lightning storm on Mt. Fuji the safest thing to do is go to the nearest hut or safety bunker. If there are no huts or bunkers within a reasonable distance, stay low and place all objects that may contain metal, like backpacks and walking poles, away from you until the storm has passed. Nevertheless, sometimes this is more easily said than done. Emergency circumstances call for quick action. One is required to use their best judgment, to read the situation and act quickly.

ICE AND SLIPPING

Ice, snow and slipping is only an issue in off-season conditions, and you should only climb in the off-season with the help of a professional mountaineer or guide. Do not attempt to climb alone in the off-season.

On the morning of Oct 28th, 2019, a young Japanese man began livestreaming his off-season climb up Mt. Fuji on YouTube.

Dramatic video footage shows the man, who

identifies himself as TEDZU, broadcasting from the snow-covered upper reaches near the summit on Monday afternoon. The video, titled "Let's Go to Snowy Mt. Fuji," shows a man climbing Mt. Fuji alone complaining of freezing temperatures, deep snow, steep slopes and slippery surfaces in the final minutes of his broadcast.

At the 10:44 mark in the clip, however, he says "This part is dangerous," as the snowy path becomes slippery. "Can't be helped, though," he continues, and immediately after, disaster strikes. 'Wait,' he says, 'I'm slipping.' The noise of his slide can be heard on the video. The fall accelerates. The video then shows him sliding feet-up, with his hiking sticks hurtling away. He could be seen tumbling downwards for several seconds before the footage ends abruptly. People watching him online then raised the alarm.

The police sent a helicopter to the location seen in the video and discovered a body two days later at about the seventh station on the Subashiri trail at Mount Fuji, at an altitude of around 9,800ft. some 2,500 ft. or 700 meters from the summit.

This was a reckless tragedy that could have been avoided. The young Japanese man was extremely underprepared for the climb and obviously had little knowledge of the off-season challenges of the mountain.

A week after this tragedy occurred, I climbed to the summit of Mt. Fuji under similar conditions with two experienced hikers. We were able to reach the summit safely without issue using the correct off-season hiking gear, taking the correct trail and practicing the correct safety precautions.

EMERGENCY EVACUATIONS

Due to the symmetrical structure and climate of the mountain, helicopters can only make emergency evacuations from as high as the 5th and 6th stations. From the summit of the mountain to the 6th stations, the only option for emergency evacuation is by bulldozer or tractor.

I once guided a fellow from Tokyo who acquired an agonizing blister on his foot during our descent (which is quite common on Mt. Fuji). After providing first aid and wrapping his blister, he asked me to call a helicopter for an evacuation. I explained the emergency evacuation guidelines. However, he was very adamant an emergency evacuation was needed. So, I called one of the mountain huts and explained the situation, requesting a bulldozer to take my client back to the 5th station. They laughed, restating the policy that bulldozer or tractor transfers were for emergencies only (i.e. broken bones, severe altitude sickness, etc.).

Finally, I called the horse vendors located at the 5th station to see if they could come and pick him up at the 7th station. They did and it ended up costing him ¥30,000 (approximately $300) for a horse ride from the 7th station to the 5th station (horse rides near the bottom are available during the climbing season on the Yoshida Route only). The moral of this story is that emergency evacuations are for life threatening injuries only! If they offered emergency evacuations for foot blisters, over half the hikers on Mt. Fuji might require evacuations.

OFFICIAL MT. FUJI GUIDES

You can always distinguish an official Mt. Fuji mountain guide from regular climbers on the mountain by their colorful armband (a different color is issued every year) and ID badges (Yoshida Route). Mountain Guides are there to ensure a safe climb and are the person climbers look to should an unexpected event happen.

To become a Mt. Fuji Guide, you need to be sponsored by one of the Mt. Fuji mountain huts and/or by the prefecture or local city office (Shizuoka side), and you need to pass Japan's intermediate first aid course.

The busiest Mt. Fuji Guides climb Mt. Fuji over 50 times in a season and some climb Mt. Fuji every day in August, the peak-climbing period. Reaching the summit before 5:00 am these guides return with their group to the 5th station between 9:00 am and 10:00 am, rest for two to three hours before starting the whole journey again with another group before noon.

The people that work on Mt. Fuji during the climbing season are a tight community: the mountain hut owners, mountain hut staff, tour operators, safety center staff and Mt. Fuji Guides all know each other in some capacity.

If you are in serious trouble and or have a serious accident on Mt. Fuji, contacting a Mt. Fuji Guide may be your best option. That Mt. Fuji Guide would be able to contact a nearby mountain hut, a safety center, or directly contact the local police department, depending on the seriousness of the injury.

Official Mt. Fuji Guides (Author and Akifumi Haneda)

CHAPTER SEVEN

GUIDED TOURS VS SELF-CLIMBS

Once you have made a commitment to climb Mt. Fuji, next you need to decide how you will make the climb itself. There are three basic climb options:

1) Group Climbing Tours
2) Private Climbing Tours
3) Self-Climbs

A guidebook like this will go a long way in your preparation to climb Mt. Fuji safely on your own; however, group and private tours can also save you a lot of time and make complicated logistics to and from Mt. Fuji hassle-free.

GROUP CLIMBING TOURS

This is probably one of the most viable options, as everything is conveniently arranged for you, all within a reasonably priced package. All you really have to worry about is getting to the designated starting point on time and making sure you have the correct equipment. The size of a group climb can be anywhere from 9 to 100 people. Group Climb Price Range: ¥25,000 ~ ¥50,000 per person depending on the tour company.

Advantage: All transportation, mountain hut accommodation, dinner, breakfast, mountain guides are included in the price.

Disadvantage: Group climbs have limited climbing dates and are usually scheduled throughout the peak climbing periods, meaning it will be crowded! If you climb during the weekends in August be prepared to wait in long line-ups and to sleep like a sardine in the overcrowded mountain huts.

PRIVATE CLIMBING TOURS

Arranging a private Mt. Fuji climb with a licensed guiding company is a very viable option. Just like group climbs, all the arrangements are prearranged for you.However, unlike group climbs you have more freedom and are not limited to certain dates and fixed schedules.

For instance, on a private 2-day climb, if your guide believes the weather on day two is unfavorable, depending on your pace, start time and where your mountain hut is situated, your guide may decide to attempt the summit on day one and stay in the mountain hut on the return. This has happened on numerous occasions, and clients are always thankful they made it to the summit on day one, when they wake up the next day to cold wind and rain. Group climbs do not allow this flexibility, which could make the difference between reaching the summit or not.

Private climbs can be arranged on almost any date to meet your schedule and can use different climbing routes (including Mt. Fuji pilgrim climbs from the base). The size of a private climb can be anywhere from one to 30 people. Private Climb Price Range: ¥40,000 ~¥200,000 per person depending on the size of the group.

Advantage: Customized to meet individual needs and schedules, all transportation, mountain hut accommodation, dinner, mountain guide and a hot spring visit after the climb are included in the price. Also at times having an English-speaking mountain guide can enhance the experience.

Disadvantage: Price

Private Climbing Tour:

"For us, hiring a private guide was by far the best decision we made. The guide allowed us to come prepared, enjoy the beauty and culture of the country and the mountain. He kept our enthusiasm in check at the start and pushed us when we needed it. All along the hike we learned little things that kept us interested and engaged. Truly an unforgettable experience!" ~ Sheila Soukup - Mt. Fuji Climbing Client.

SELF-CLIMBS

Self-climbs are by far the cheapest option and you are given freedom to arrange the trip on your own time schedule; however, you are left to organize everything yourself and with limited or no Japanese language skills this can be extremely challenging, as well as really time consuming.

First you have to get to Mt. Fuji on your own. This includes making your own train or bus reservations and coordinating all your own time schedules. For a two-day climb, you will need to make your own mountain hut reservation.

Note: Climbing with a friend is highly recommended, just in case you run into trouble on the mountain. If this is not possible, joining a group tour would be a safer climb option.

Size of Group: Depends on you.
Self-Climb Price Range: ¥15,000~¥25,000 per person depending on transportation.

Advantage: The price and you can choose different ascending and descending trails (for example up the Yoshida Trail and down the Subashiri Trail), as you are not committed to the same start and end points like many group tours.

Disadvantage: You have to arrange everything on your own, from transportation to and from the mountain, food, mountain hut accommodation, hiking rentals, transportation to the hot spring after the climb. It is all up to you and if you run into trouble on the mountain, there is no translator or guide to assist you.

CHAPTER EIGHT

CLIMB OPTIONS

Similar to choosing a self, private or group climbing tour, you must also choose the duration of your Mt. Fuji climb. And again there are three basic options, plus, the decision to climb during the official climbing season or during the off-season.

- Two-Day Climbs
- Day Climbs
- Night Climbs
- Off-Season Climbs

TWO-DAY CLIMBS

It seems obvious that the safest and most sensible way to climb Mt. Fuji is to take two days. This allows you adequate time to rest, recover your strength, catch your breath, eat, sleep, and adjust to the altitude before getting up in the early morning to push to the summit to witness the sunrise.

The extra day also allows you the chance to experience a night at an authentic Japanese style mountain hut, a chance to meet the mountain hut staff and a chance to meet other climbers from around the world staying there. Most tour companies only offer two-day climbing tours.

A day or night climb are alternatives and may be the only option if you are unable to secure a mountain hut reservation or join a climbing tour.

A one-day climb, without a mountain hut stay, can be done at night or during the day, by hiking all through the night to catch the morning sunrise (some tour companies still offer night climbing tours) or during the day to enjoy the sunset from the summit.

Compared to a two-day climb, a one-day climb can be very exhausting and twice as dangerous. The likelihood of altitude sickness greatly increases the faster you hike up the mountain. However, saying this, if one is well prepared and goes about it safely, a one-day climb can be an achievable and an enjoyable way to climb Mt. Fuji.

DAY CLIMBS

Climbing during the day can present a distinctive set of problems for hikers. The extreme heat greatly increases dehydration and heat stroke risk. Also, the sun can be merciless even if you feel like it's too cold to get burned.

A sunhat and sunscreen are essential items for daytime climbs. And even for day climbs, it is important to bring a headlight or flashlight as day climbs can take anywhere between ten to twelve hours. Plus, depending on the trail you may not return to the 5th station until after dark.

Your start time will depend on which trail you choose. The longer Subashiri and Yoshida Trails require more time. It is recommended that you start your climb on these routes by 6:00 am. If you are doing a day climb from the Fujinomiya Route, start no later than 7:00 am to give you lots of time to reach the summit before sunset.

Note: It is highly recommended you Do Not use the Gotemba trail for one-day climbs, due to its long time-consuming distance.

The huts on the summit close by 5:00 pm, so if you would like to have a nice bowl of ramen at the top, you must reach the top before 5:00 pm. If you are fortunate enough to reach the summit before 3:00 pm, try walking around the crater in order to explore the vast panoramic views.

NIGHT CLIMBS

Night climbs (or bullet climbs as they are referred to in Japan) consist of climbing all through the night to catch the morning sunrise. This type of climb pose new challenges, as it is cold and dark, and as you climb through the night it disrupts your routine sleeping pattern, which adds to your exhaustion and lack of energy.

Night climb hazards include unforeseen rocks, cold winds, and sleep deprivation, which all increase the chance of making errors. Wearing warmer clothes and bringing a headlight or flashlight is compulsory.

Due to the increased injuries caused by night climbs, the Japanese Ministry of Environment (MOE) started a "stop bullet climbing" campaign and it may not be long before they regulate the number of bullet climbers allowed to climb at night or ban night climbs altogether. MOE has issued the following warnings:

RISKS/DANGERS OF BULLET CLIMBING

Climbers who have not properly slept are more prone to injuries and illness due to fatigue.

14% of bullet climbers (5% of standard climbers) give up climbing to the summit because they became ill.

The number of bullet climbers who seek help at first-aid centers is three times higher than that of standard climbers.

COLDNESS

Temperatures at the summit may drop to below freezing even in July and August.

FALLING ROCKS

Due to darkness, climbers are more likely to cause rocks to fall—a potential danger to other climbers below.

Start time will depend on what route you select. For the Yoshida Trail, starting your climb from the 5th station between 8:00 pm and 9:00 pm should give you lots of time to reach the summit by sunrise (at a reasonably safe pace), leaving lots of time for rests and waits at the crowded logjams near the top.

During August weekends and the Obon holiday period in mid-August, as many as 5,000 climbers can be seen on the top of the Yoshida Trail at the same time on any given night!

OFF-SEASON CLIMBS

Is it safe to climb Mt. Fuji in the off-season? I am often asked this question. The politically correct answer is; **"Generally speaking it is not recommended to climb Mt. Fuji in the off-season"**. However, when asked this question by experienced climbers, I reply. **"When in the off-season do you want to climb?"** As a general rule the further away from the climbing season, you get the greater the danger. When climbing Mt. Fuji, a great deal depends on the weather. It is difficult to approximate when the best date to climb is, as the climate is forever changing. You may have a dreadful awful rainy/ windy day in August and a beautiful sunny day in October. The weather on the day of your climb plays a large part of how risky your climb may be.

I have climbed Mt. Fuji from April to November and some of my most pleasant climbs have come during the off-season. Doing a one-day climb in May, June or late September with the right equipment, right weather and the right friend can be extremely enjoyable.

Nevertheless, the harsh reality is every single year overconfidence results in fatalities on Mt. Fuji and almost all of these deaths occur in the off-season.

Climbing Mt. Fuji during the official climbing season and for a couple of months before or after poses a certain amount of risk; however, climbing during the winter off-season after October greatly increases the risks, as the dangers and hazards rise.

Unless you are a professional climber, I would unequivocally avoid climbing Mt. Fuji during the deep winter months (any month from November to April). As an example, during these months, wind chill temperatures of -40C are common above the 8th station and all trails from November to May are completely covered in snow and ice, so it is easy to get lost. Mt. Fuji occasionally has horrendous winds (40m/sec~50m/sec), and there are avalanche threats especially in the winter and spring.

OFF-SEASON CLIMBING TIPS

Despite the risks and warnings, some people will undoubtedly choose to climb Mt. Fuji in the winter off-season anyway. For those people who ignore all the warnings and accept all personal responsibility for their own safety, here are some off-season climbing tips:

1. **Use the Fujinomiya Route.** This is the most popular off-season route, as it is the shortest route to the summit. There is only one-way up and one-way down, so you are less likely to get lost compared to the other routes. As this is the preferred off-season route, most likely you will not be alone, especially if you climb on a sunny weekend.

2. **Use the tractor trails.** Using the tractor/bulldozer trails is strictly forbidden during climbing season, however once all the mountain huts are closed, these trails are unoccupied and are your best option for a quick descent.

3. **Employ a professional guide** and bring the following equipment; crampons (twelve nails and well-shaped), an alpine ice axe, climbing rope, a pair of ski poles, food, water, thermos and hot drinks (coffee, soup, etc.), heavy weather wear, a warm cap, snow goggles, and a flashlight.

4. **Register with the local police** before climbing in the deep off-season. Both Yamanashi and Shizuoka Mountain Safety Authorities do not

recommend you climb during the off-season. However, if you do, they ask that you submit a climbing plan before you climb. The climbing plan must list the route, schedule, equipment, group members and who to contact in case of emergency. A climbing plan form is available at the back of this guidebook and can be obtained from the official climbing Fujisan website and faxed to the location depending on your expected climbing route.

Submission of Mt. Fuji Climbing Plan

Download: http://fujisan-climb.jp/en/risk/guidelines.html

Fax Numbers

Yoshida Trail Fax: 0555-22-0110
Subashiri Trail Fax: 0550-76-3050
Gotemba Trail Fax: 0550-82-4523
Fujinomiya Trail Fax: 0544-22-1385

There are some mountain huts on Mt. Fuji that remain open from June until the middle of October (The Taiyo-Kan Hut at the 7th station on the Subashiri Route and the Unkaiso and Hoeisanso Mountain Huts at the 6th station on the Fujinomiya Route). Public services such as toilets, safety centers, first aid facilities are closed and all the location markers and signposts are removed once the official climbing season ends. Depending on how deep in the off-season you intend to climb, the risks change greatly. See a general guide for off-season climbing risks on the next page.

OFF-SEASON CLIMBING RISKS

*	Sept/Oct: Three mountain huts remain open until the middle of October. Typhoon season (rain/wind/thunder/lightning).
**	Nov: Exceptionally windy with freezing climate (fresh snow).
***	Dec-April: Extremely freezing climate with horrendous subzero winds (fresh snow and ice).
**	May: Exceptionally windy and cold, 8th station to summit covered in ice; possibility of avalanche.
*	June: Snow starts to melt, possibility of avalanche; one mountain hut is open on the Subashiri Route.

*	Moderate Risk: A one or two-day climb is possible in the company of a professional guide.
**	High Risk: Only professional mountaineers should attempt with a guide.
***	Extremely Dangerous: Do not attempt to climb during this period.

Note: If you are in Japan during the winter off-season, and want to do some hiking, some great alternatives to a Mt. Fuji summit climb are a Mt. Takao, Mt. Jinba or Hachijo Fuji hike (see Tokyo Warm Up Hikes in Chapter Nine).

CHAPTER NINE

CLIMB PREPARATION

PRE-CLIMB TRAINING

Preparation is key! Starting a fitness program to train for your climb may be one of the best things you can do. Start your training well in advance of your climb. It is wise to seek your doctor's approval and the guidance of a fitness trainer.

STEP 1: ASSESS YOUR FITNESS LEVEL

Some of us kid ourselves as to how fit we actually are, but undoubtedly most have some sense of how fit we really are. Regardless of your fitness level, some training is required. If you have an ongoing training routine and/or play sports regularly, you may only require more specific training. In this case, your training will need to be adjusted to match the specific physical requirements of climbing Mt. Fuji. If you do not do any training, the climb will be challenging. If you do not have a fitness routine of any type, the first step may be to evaluate your current fitness level to give you a benchmark against which to measure your progress.

STEP 2: DESIGN YOUR FITNESS PROGRAM FOR HIKING

Basically, climbing Mt. Fuji places a lot of physical stress on your body; hence, the better these stresses on your body can be duplicated before the climb -- the better your body can adapt to the stress during your climb. Cardiovascular fitness is simply not enough. People who successfully run marathons fail to summit high-altitude peaks. Training emphasis needs to be on building the physical conditioning necessary to ascend 1,500 meters (5,000 ft.) of elevation while carrying seven to ten kilos (15-20 lbs.) up slopes with as much as a 40-degree steep. The physical capabilities necessary to successfully climb Mt. Fuji are discussed below.

Cardiovascular Fitness – The ability to take in and supply oxygen to your body. This is the most important element necessary to climb Mt. Fuji. The effect of altitude sickness is the same, it doesn't matter how great of shape an individual is in. So, it stands to reason, the more oxygen the body can send to its muscles -- the better the body will function.

Strength (Lower/Upper Body and Core) – Strength means the ability to move quickly while maintaining stability, endurance and balance. The calves, hips, thigh muscles and hamstrings are all involved in ascending and descending steep slopes. Strength endurance is required in the legs and hips. Developing strength in the upper back and shoulders helps with tasks such as carrying your pack and using trekking poles effectively.

Acclimatization Fitness – The ability to adapt quickly to elevation changes to enhance the lungs ability to cope with the challenges of altitude.

STEP 3: GETTING STARTED

Adjust your training program, depending on how much time you have, from when you decide to climb Mt. Fuji to when you actually climb the mountain.
  Integrating the above physical capabilities into your fitness program will help prepare you to climb Mt. Fuji. See some specific training recommendations below.

• Cardiovascular Conditioning
• Trail Running
• Inclined Treadmill Running
• Step Aerobics Classes

  Swimming, biking and skipping are great aerobic options for the beginning stages of training. As you get closer to the trip include activities which replicate steep climbing motions so your spine and legs replicate the climbing action. Training three times a week for 30 to 50 minutes will help you improve your overall cardiovascular capacity.
  Strength Conditioning – Training with free weights or gym machines will help you build overall strength. Remember, your shoulders and lower back will need to be strong to carry the necessary supplies on the climb. The following full body eight-exercise strength workout covers the major muscles used when climbing.

FULL BODY STRENGTH WORKOUT

- Squats and Lunges (Legs)
- Back Extensions (Lower Back)
- Stiff-Legged Dead Lift (Lower Back)
- Seated Cable Rows (Upper Back)
- Overhead Press (Shoulders)
- Biceps Curls and Triceps Dips (Arms)
- Sit-ups and Twists – Incline sit-ups and Seated Twists using Medicine Ball (Torso and Abdominals)

At the start of strength training, proper form is important in order to prevent injury. Completing two sets of each of the exercises above for 10-12 repetitions. As you continue to train, you will change the focus from form to building strength. At this time, lower repetitions to 6-8 using heavier weights.

Finally, a month before the climb, change your weekly workout schedule to rotate between both low and high repetitions to focus on strength endurance (see sample-training schedule). During any training stage, always be sure you maintain proper form in order to prevent injury.

Climb Conditioning – Climb specific training for quicker elevation adaptation.

Options include:
- Hiking outdoor trails and or hills with a weighted pack.
- Walking up and down stairs or stadium bleacher with a weighted pack.
- Walking on Stairmaster with the incline set at five or higher with weighted pack.

Pack: Start off light and gradually increase the weight in the pack until you feel comfortable carrying around a 20-pound (seven to ten kilos) pack.

SAMPLE TRAINING SCHEDULE

A sample week of training one month prior to your climb might look like the chart below. Be sure to include at least one recovery day per week. Always pay close attention to your body.

Day	Climb Conditioning	Strength	Cardio	Flexibility
Mon		Full Body 10-12 reps	For 30 min (1 of 3 options)	10 min Stretch at end
Tues	Hiking, Stairs or Stairmaster (with Pack)			10 min Stretch at end
Wed		Full Body 6-8 reps	For 50 min (1 of 3 options)	10 min Stretch at end
Thru	Hiking, Stairs or Stairmaster (with Pack)			10 min Stretch at end
Fri		Full Body 10-12 reps	For 30 min (1 of 3 options)	10 min Stretch at end
Sat	Hiking, Stairs or Stairmaster (with Pack)			10 min Stretch at end
Sun	Rest Day			

The goal of climbing Mt. Fuji is usually motivation enough; however, keeping a training log of your progress and identifying your improvements is also very helpful.

TOKYO WARM UP HIKES

If you are in Tokyo and have time before your Mt. Fuji hike, I recommend one of the following low altitude hikes as a way to prepare for the Mt. Fuji climb and a lovely way to enjoy more of Japan's beautiful surrounding nature.

Mt. Takao is one of the closest green parklands to the big metropolis of Tokyo offering beautiful scenery, interesting temples and other attractions. Many people are already aware of Tokyo's Mt. Takao as a famous hiking spot. It became well known after receiving a Michelin Green Guide three-star rating.

Mt. Takao is easy to access via the Keio train line from Shinjuku. Due to its proximity to central Tokyo the hike is very popular and can get crowded on weekends. Mt. Takao stands at 599 meters (1965 ft.) and has a number of hiking trails to the summit. The hike on Trial Number 1 only takes about 90 minutes to the summit. If you do this hike in preparation for climbing Mt. Fuji adding a weighted pack is suggested.

Mt. Jinba, located along the borders of Tokyo and Kanagawa Prefecture, is not as famous as Mt. Takao, however, Mt. Jinba is listed as one of Japan's best mountains to hike and is more challenging to climb than Mt. Takao. Mt. Jinba is a much steeper climb standing at around 857 meters (2811 ft.) tall. It takes about 2 hours to reach the summit.

The trek starts on a paved road. After about 1.5 kms the entrance to the nature trail will appear on your left. You can either take the nature trail to the summit or continue on the paved road that leads all the way to the Wada Pass. This trail connects to a nature path for the last 20 minutes of the hike to the summit.

To access Mt. Jinba, from Takao Station (Chuo Line) take the Nishi Tokyo Bus from the #1 bus stop all the way to the final stop at Mt. Jinba Kogen Shita. On a clear day, you can view Mt. Fuji in the distance from the summit of both Mt. Takao and Mt. Jinba. Also, you can actually climb both mountains and hike from one to the other in one day. This 7-hour hike is not as challenging as a Mt. Fuji climb, but it is a longer hike (18.5 km, 11.5 mi). It is also easy to get lost if you cannot read Japanese, therefore, it is recommended that you go with someone that has done the trail before or get a guide to accompany you. It is not recommended you try this trail on your own.

Mt. Takao (Route #1)

MT. HACHIJO-FUJI

Last summer I decided to take a short rest from climbing Mt. Fuji to escape to the sea. I flew 300 kms directly south of Tokyo to the tiny island of Hachijo. Unexpectedly I discovered on Hachijo-jima (as it is called in Japanese)a volcanic peak that has the same iconic cone structure as Mt. Fuji. The name of this mountain coincidently is called Hachijo-Fuji. I could not pass on the opportunity to climb this smaller version of Mt. Fuji and was glad I did. The elevation of Mt. Hachijo-Fuji is only 854 meters (2,802 ft.) high and the terrain is covered with lush forest and green shrubs and the views of the surrounding sea from the summit rim are simply spectacular.

The island is part of the Izu peninsula volcanic island chain and officially under the jurisdiction of Tokyo Prefecture. The Island is included in the Fuji-Hakon-Izu National Park. The direct flight from Haneda Airport to Hachijo-jima Airport takes one hour and there are three flights daily.

You can drive to the 7th station by car and park by the side of the road than take the path to the summit. It takes about one hour in total to climb to the summit of Hachijo-Fuji from here. The hike is exactly 1,280 steps on a fairly steep path to the top of the trail, then another 30 minutes along the rim to the mountain summit.

The crater is full of plants and small trees; the diameter is 400 meters with a depth of around 50 meters. A rim hike takes about an hour to walk the complete loop.

There are two paths that lead into the crater; the first is a fairly easy 10-minute hike to the Sengen Shrine gate. The second is a windy trek through a shrub covered trail that is difficult to find at times. The hidden trail goes deep into the center of the crater where there are several fresh water ponds. If you have a couple of extra days in Tokyo, and can make the short flight to Hachijo-jima this would make for an exceptional island hiking adventure.

Mt.Hachijo-Fuji

CHAPTER TEN

MT. FUJI ONSENS & PICTURES

MT. FUJI ONSENS

After climbing Mt. Fuji there is no better reward than relaxing in a natural hot spring. The volcanic area around Mt. Fuji is home to hundreds and some of the best natural hot springs or "onsens" as they are referred to in Japan.

Appreciating a Japanese onsen is in itself a cultural experience. This is even more so after climbing Mt. Fuji when you need it the most. Relaxing your sore muscles in the healing volcanic mineral water leaves you rejuvenated and refreshed.

For local Japanese climbers enjoying an onsen after each climb is a necessary routine and as important as the climb itself. Every local Mt. Fuji climbing tour includes a stop at an onsen after each climb to relax.

For many first-time visitors to Japan, entering an onsen is a somewhat unfamiliar experience that involves bathing nude with others of the same sex in hot mineral water.

Unwilling to try this new experience some visitors decide to skip the onsen altogether, which is a real shame as the alternative after a Mt. Fuji climb is to spend the next several hours on a bus sitting next to others, dirty, smelly and sore. If you get a chance I highly recommend trying an onsen experience after climbing Mt. Fuji. Your body will be grateful you did. Below is a list of preferred Mt. Fuji onsens that I regularly visit during the climbing season. The onsen I visit largely depends on the climbing route taken.

Hana no Yu Onsen (Fujinomiya)
Nearest Route: Fujinomiya Route
Access: Shin-Fuji Stations (10 mins)
Specialties: Various onsens, Hotel, Rental Shop
Web: tokinosumika.com/hananoyu/ (Japanese)
Bus: Fujikyu bus from Shin-Fuji and Fujinomiya Stations, regular stop on route to the Fujinomiya 5th Station.

This onsen is popular with Fujinomiya Route climbers, as it offers easy access from Shin-Fuji Station via the Fujikyu Bus. During the summer climbing season, Mr. Takashima, a sales representative from Hana no Yu hands out discount tickets at the Fujinomiya 5th Station and sometimes he even climbs Mt. Fuji and hand delivers discount tickets to all the mountain huts on the Fujinomiya Route.

This onsen facility is huge. They have over ten types of onsens, including a salt water onsen, similar to the dead sea, a kusatsu onsen which imports minimal water from the kusatsu region of Japan, as well as saunas, steam rooms, massage areas and a restaurant. Hana no Yu also has several reasonably priced single and twin rooms available for you to stay the night. During the climbing season the facility has a hiking rental shop to cover all your basic equipment needs.

Tenkei Onsen (Oyama)
Nearest Route: Subashiri Climbing Route
Access: Gotemba Station (25 mins)
Specialties: Mixed Bath, Hotel, SwimSuits, Dr. Fish
Bus: Highway bus from Gotemba Station
Web: Tokinosumika.com/tenkei/ (Japanese)

This onsen is located next to the highway entrance point of the Subashiri Route. This is one of the few onsens that offers a mixed bath area that allows you to wear swimsuits so you can enjoy the experience with friends and family. If you forgot your swimsuit, no problem, they also offer swimsuit rentals.

Found in the mixed onsen area is a footbath that includes a fish spa treatment, known as Doctor Fish. Basically, this involves placing your feet in a footbath filled with toothless garra rufa fish that clean the dead skin off your feet. It is very popular. This onsen also has several sensibly priced rooms for you to stay the night.

Hana no Yu Onsen (Fujinomiya)

Otainai Onsen (Gotemba)
Nearest Routes: Fujinomiya/Gotemba Routes
Access: Gotemba Station (20 mins)
Bus: Free shuttle service to/from Gotemba Station
Specialties: Onsen with a view of Fuji
Web: otainai-onsen.gr.jp (Japanese)

Located in Gotemba, Otainai Onsen is one of the most inexpensive onsens in the area. It is located not far from the Gotemba and Fujinomiya Route access points. Not openly stated anywhere, this onsen seems to allow access to visitors who have tattoos, though as a rule guests with tattoos are generally forbidden in public onsens. Tattooed guests have entered without issue and I have even seen the occasional tattooed Japanese in this onsen. Let us hope this is policy and just not an oversight by the staff.

Fuji Yurari Onsen (Narusawa - Kawaguchi)
Nearest Route: Yoshida Climbing Route
Specialties: Onsen with view of Fuji
Access: Kawaguchi Station (20 mins)
Bus: shuttle service to/from Kawaguchi Station
Web: fuji-yurari.jp (Japanese)

The appeal of the Otainai Onsen is on a clear day from this onsen there is a great view of Mt. Fuji. So while you soak and relax in the onsen you can enjoy a view of the mountain you just concurred.

MT. FUJI PICTURES

Kage Fuji

Kage Fuji (Meaning Shadow Fuji) is the name given to the huge triangular shadow cast by Mt. Fuji that covers the lower clouds and regions when seen from the peak of Mt. Fuji.

Mt. Fuji Night View

On a chance, rare occasion during the summer climbing season the clear night sky, warm temperature and bright mood permit the stars, surrounding cities, lakes, and ocean below to be visibly seen from the mountain. On these nights, a climb to the summit can be safely made, yet anticipating these rare nights is difficult.

Stretching

To prevent injury and cramping stretching is an essential aspect of any pre-climbing routine. Stretching before and during your climb to the summit will help reduce muscle cramping during the difficult descent. Also after a strenuous day of hiking, stretching helps reduce muscle soreness.

Mountain Hut Lodgings

Mountain hut lodgings on Mt. Fuji are fairly simple, offering dormitory style bunk beds with blankets and sleeping bags. Do not expect hotel type conditions with separate rooms. Reservations are taken care of if you join a group or private tour. However, if you plan your own climb you will have to make your own mountain hut reservation. A list of mountain huts, including contact information is available on pages 47 ~ 49.

Mt. Fuji's Kengamine Marker

This is the marker you will see if you reach the highest peak on Mt. Fuji. The literal translation of the Japanese inscription written on the marker is: "Japan's highest peak Mt. Fuji Kengamine 3,776 meters".

Mt. Fuji # 1 (Author and Mr. Jitsukawa)

At 77 years old, Mr. Jitsukawa is the most famous guide on the mountain with over 2,200 climbs to his credit. Mr. Jitsukawa proudly displays the number of climbs he has completed on his hat, updating the number with each new climb. Besides guiding numerous famous people to the summit, he has written a guidebook on climbing Mt. Fuji. Next year he will attempt to climb Mt. Everest for the fourth time..

Sand Run - Subashiri Route (Author)

The sand run on the descending Subashiri Route is a straight gravel down slope between the 7th and 6th stations. There is a much longer sand run referred to as the great sand run on the Gotemba Route descending trail, covering a third of the mountain between the 7th and 5th stations. By taking huge leaping strides you can cover in minutes the same distances that it took hours to hike up.

Mt. Fuji in the Off-Season

On any given sunny weekend in May or June, Mt. Fuji's Fujinomiya Route could be mistaken for a popular ski resort, as many climbers scale the side of the mountain with crampons clamped on their hiking shoes and skis or snowboards attached to their backpacks for a quick descent. Refer to Chapter Eight "Climb Options" for more information about off-season climbs.

Mt. Fuji's Summit Crater

On a clear day, you can look right into the crater from the summit of Mt. Fuji. Mt. Fuji's summit crater is approximately 600 meters (1,968 ft.) wide and 200 meters (656 ft.) deep. Circling the entire crater takes about 90 minutes. Climbing into the crater itself is extremely dangerous and should never be attempted. Evacuation from inside the crater would be next to impossible.

The Aokigahara Forest (Shoji Trail)

The Aokigahara Forest also known as the "Sea of trees" has the unfortunate distinction of being called a haunted forest. Ever since the novel 'Kuroi Jukai' by Seicho Matsumoto was published in 1960, in which the characters are focused on joint-suicide in the forest, the popularity of the so-called suicide forest has increased among those determined to take their final walk. These events have inspired numerous horror movies centered around the forest. However contrary to popular belief, the Aokigahara Forest is a beautiful dense porous lava based forest with hundreds of unique tree moles and ice caves. The hiking trail starting from lake Shoji-ko has been revitalized in recent years, continues upward until it crosses the Fuji Subaru Line Toll Road at the 3rd station-Jukaidai parking area and then finally intersects with the Fuji Subaru Line 5th Station.

The Fuji Subaru Line 5th Station

The Fuji Subaru Line 5th Station is the most popular and largest of the four 5th stations on Mt. Fuji. It has several restaurants, souvenir shops, coin lockers and a shrine. It is the only 5th station where you can rent a horse to go on a scenic ride. Every day in the summer hundreds of tourists visit this 5th station as it is on the popular Mt. Fuji and Hakone day tour route. These tourists come to enjoy the view, shops and food, but not to climb the mountain.

The Subashiri 5th Station

The Subashiri 5th Station renowned for its wild mushrooms consists of two family-run shops. The first shop on the left when you approach the trail is Kikuya. The friendly Kikuya shop has a rich history of over 350 years and was formerly located at the second station and accessible by horse before the road was paved to the present location. The second shop, Higashi-Fuji Sanso was given permission to build, after the road to the 5th station was completed and the two family-run shops have endured obsessively ever since. Unknown to the casual visitor, this 5th station is Mt. Fuji's version of the Hatfield-McCoy feud.

MT. FUJI CLIMBING ETIQUETTES

Mt. Fuji is the center of the Fuji-Hakone-Izu National Park. It is an historic site with extraordinary scenic beauty. The following is a list of common climbing rules and warnings. Certain acts are legally prohibited in designated areas.

Ascending: On the mountain, people ascending take precedence over people descending. So if there is a stand off on the trail -- please yeild to the people climbing up.

Breaks: Take your rest breaks on the side of the trail so as not to impede other people climbing.

Camping: Absolutely no camping is allowed on the mountain. (Note: Around the base of Mt. Fuji there are several camping sites.)

Fires: Absolutely no camp fires are allowed on the mountain. (Note: Around the base of Mt. Fuji there are several camping sites that allow fires.)

Garbage: There are no garbage cans on Mt. Fuji. You must carry your garbage with you at all times and take it with you when you leave the mountain.

Mountain Souvenirs: You are prohibited from taking any rocks or plants from the mountain home with you: "Take only Pictures, Leave only Footprints".

Rocks (Edge of Trail): To prevent falling rocks, do not climb or sit on the edge of the trails, especially during the descent as this can start a rockslide that could injure others. This may go without saying, but do not kick or throw rocks off the mountain, at times young children have to be reminded of this.

Tractor Routes: Have you ever wondered how they get all the supplies and materials up Mt. Fuji? Well, there are tractors and bulldozers that carry supplies up to the summit and mountain huts. On the mountain there are paths exclusively for these supply bulldozers and tractors. They are not always clearly marked and occasionally intersect with the actual climbing trails. Using these routes during the climbing season is strictly forbidden.

Trails: Do not deviate from the trails; always climb within the designated ropes.

Toilets: Proper climbing etiquette requires everyone to bring back what they took with them. This includes your excrement. In the off-season this issue increases, as there are limited or no toilets available. It is good mountain manners to scoop and bag your excrement and take it with you to dispose of later if you are unable to use a washroom

Washrooms: Please bring coins for the washrooms. You are asked to pay ¥200~¥500 fee for using the washrooms. Some mountain huts now have a pay gate while others have a staff member guarding the washrooms 24 hours a day. So, if you think you can sneak into the washrooms without paying – think again.

Drones: From all 5th Stations up to the summit, Mt. Fuji has implemented a strict no fly zone.

FINAL WORDS

A famous Japanese proverb says: **"He who does not climb Mt. Fuji is a fool, but he who climbs Mt. Fuji more than once is a bigger fool."**

Most people in Japan and a number of people abroad dream of climbing Mt. Fuji (and watching a stunning sunrise from the summit) at least once in their lifetime.

Therefore, making the most of the experience is essential. If you desire a great experience, careful preparation is necessary. Decide what type of climb you want: one-day or two-day. Decide if you will join a group, hire a guide or go on your own. Reserve a mountain hut if required. Take the time to train and secure proper hiking equipment. Remember to climb at a slow pace, give yourself a lot of time and try using the techniques outlined in this guide to ensure a safe climbing experience.

The purpose of this guidebook is to assist in creating a safer and more memorable Mt. Fuji climbing experience for climbers. If you consider all or even some of the techniques or hints outlined within this guidebook your chances for success will significantly increase and this will contribute to a more enjoyable experience on Mt. Fuji.

Pushing your body to the limit to reach Mt. Fuji's peak is extremely gratifying. As you stare down at the world below and watch the sunrise you feel a huge sense of accomplishment when you realize just how high you have climbed. It is truly a satisfying and memorable experience. Sometimes, on a clear day from the summit, it is a spiritual experience.

Thank you for taking the time to read this guidebook. I hope you have a safe and amazing, once in a lifetime experience climbing Mt. Fuji. I look forward to seeing you on the mountain!

Sunrise from 9th Station - Photograph by Taishi Takahashi

APPENDICES

MT. FUJI GLOSSARY LIST

Abunai — Danger – "Be Careful".

Dangan Tozan — Literally means "Bullet Climb," a night climb without a rest.

Diamond Fuji — The name given to the view of the sun as it meets the summit of Mt. Fuji around the winter solstice – seen from Yamanakako and Tanukiko.

Red Fuji — Observed in the morning from late summer to early autumn.

Kage Fuji — The shadow cast by Mt. Fuji as seen from the peak.

Sakasa Fuji — Upside Down Fuji, the reflection of Mt. Fuji that can be seen on one of the lakes at the base of the mountain.

Go-Gome — 5th stage or 5th station.

Roku-Gome — 6th stage or 6th station.

Nana-Gome — 7th stage or 7th station.

Hachi-Gome	8th stage or 8th station.
Kyu-Gome	9th stage or 9th station.
Gezan	Descend – down the mountain.
Goraiko	A special name for a sunrise viewed from a mountain summit.
Guchi	Entrance like in "Yoshida Guchi," literally means Yoshida Trailhead.
Hachi	Literally means "Bowl". It is used to describe the crater.
Hayashi Rice	Literary means "hash & rice" a type of beef stew served with rice.
Higaeri	One-Day Climb – there and back in one day.
Kengamine	Actually means crater edge – It is the name of the highest of the eight summit peaks of Mt. Fuji.
Konnichiwa	Hello in Japanese, a common greeting when hiking Mt. Fuji.
Kusushi Shrine	One of two Mt. Fuji summit shrines.
Mannenyuki	Literally means "10,000 Year Snow," refers to Mt. Fuji's glacier.
Miso Shiru	Miso Soup, soup made with miso and vegetables.
Ochuudo	Literally means "the middle road," name of the trail that circles Mt. Fuji.

Ohachi-Meguri	Loop hike around the rim of the summit crater.
Omoteguchi	The front entrance of the mountain, refers to the Fujinomiya Trail.
Osunabashiri	"Great Sand Run" on the Gotemba Trail.
Raku Seki	Falling rocks.
Sanchou or Chojo	Summit of the mountain.
Sengentaisha Okumiya Shrine	One of two Mt. Fuji summit shrines.
Tengu	The red faced, log-nosed, winged mythical goblin who lives deep in the mountain.
Tonjiru	Soup made with pork and vegetables.
Tozan	Ascend – go up the mountain.
Yakiin	Literally means "Burn Stamp". The stamp burnt into wooden walking sticks.
Yama Girl	Literally means "mountain girl," it refers to female Japanese outdoor clothing fashion used for mountain climbing (staple of Yama girl fashion are the colorful tights/legging and a skirt).
Yama Goya	Literally means "small mountain house," a mountain hut.

FINAL WARMING LIST

Warning: If you do not want to climb Mt. Fuji – Do not climb Mt. Fuji.

Warning: Day climbs, when doing a day climb do not start any later than 8:00 am (starting from 5th station

Warning: Do not attempt to climb at night or day without some type of light.

Warning: Night climbs, when doing a night climb do not start any later than 9:00 pm (starting from 5th station).

Warning: Do not attempt to climb Mt. Fuji immediately after arriving at the 5th station.

Warning: In case of a lightning storm, go to the nearest hut or safety bunker a.s.a.p.

Warning: Do not attempt to climb in the early off-season without a guide (Oct, Nov, May, June).

Warning: Do not attempt to climb in the deep off-season period (Dec-April).

ALTITUDE SICKNESS PREVENTION LIST

- Give your body time to acclimatize to the changing altitude. (one-hour at 5th Station)

- Hike slowly up the mountain.

- Drink plenty of water (see dehydration section).

- Eat lots of high fat foods, (chocolate, nuts) which are easy to digest.

- Avoid red meats; the digestive process slows down at high altitudes.

- Avoid caffeine and alcohol as these can increase the likelihood of dehydration.

- Use the pressure-breathing technique to increase oxygen intake.

- If required take Diamox or other altitude sickness medication prescribed by a doctor.

EMERGENCY CONTACT NUMBERS

FIRST AID CENTERS (SUMMER ONLY)

Mt. Fuji 8th Station (Fujinomiya) First Aid-Center 0544-22-2238
Mt. Fuji 8th Station (Yoshida) First Aid-Center 0544-24-6223
Mt. Fuji 7th Station (Yoshida) First Aid-Center 0555-24-6520

GUIDANCE CENTERS (SUMMER ONLY)

Guidance Center (Yamanashi 5th Station) 0555-72-1477
Safety Guidance Center (Yoshida Route 6th Station) 0555-24-6223
Guidance Center (Fujinomiya 5th Station) 0544-22-2239
Guidance Center (Subashiri 5th Station) 0550-76-6114

INFORMATION CENTERS

Fuji Visitor Center (Mt. Fuji Yamanashi) 0555-72-0259
Kawaguchiko Tourist Center 0555-72-6700
Fujiyoshida Tourist Center 0555-22-7000
Yamanakako Tourist Visitor Center 0555-62-3100

MT. FUJI POLICE STATIONS

Fujinomiya Police Station 0544-23-0110
Fuji Police Station 0545-51-0110
Gotemba Police Station 0550-84-0110
Fujiyoshida Police Station 0555-22-0110

MT. FUJI ACCESS INFORMATION

TRAIN TRANSPORTATION

JR Central English Website (access, routes, schedules, fares)
https://global.jr-central.co.jp/en/

JR East Railway Company English Website (access, routes, schedules, fares) http://www.jreast.co.jp/e/index.html

Odakyu Electric Railway English Website (access, routes, schedules, fares) http://www.odakyu.jp/english/traffic/ (03-3481-0066)

JR Tokai Railway 050-3772-3910
Fuji Kyuko Railway 0555-22-7133
Izuhakone Railway 055-977-1207
Shizuoka Railway 054-254-5114

BUS TRANSPORTATION

Fujikyu English Website (access, routes, schedules, fares)
http://bus-en.fujikyu.co.jp/highway/

Keihin Kyuko Bus - Haneda Airport to Mt. Fuji (access, routes, schedules, fares)
http://hnd-bus.com/route/kawaguchiko.html

Fujikyu Shizuoka Bus (Fujinomiya Trail) 0545-71-2495
Fuji Kyuko Bus (Gotemba Trail, Subashiri Trail) 0550-82-133
Fujikyu Yamanashi Bus (Yoshida Trail) 0555-72-6873
Keio Expressway Bus (reservation center) 03-5376-2222
Fujikyu Expressway Bus (reservation center) 0555-72-5111

REFERENCES

Sources for this book include numerous conversations with clients and other Mt. Fuji Guides. A few of the key publications include the following:

- Douill, John. (March 2013) Fuji: Seven Sacred Trails. Greenshinto.com http://greenshinto.com/wp/2013/03/31/fuji-seven-sacred-trails/

- Fujikyuko Co. Ltd., Mt. Fuji Explorer, 2013. http://mtfuji-jp.com/

- Fujiyoshida City Official Website, 2006. https://www.city.fujiyoshida.yamanashi.jp/

- Johnson, J. Leslie. Basic Mountain Safety Canmore, Alberta: Altitude Publishing, 2000.

- Official Web Site for Mt. Fuji Climbing - MOF, 2014. http://fujisan-climb.jp/en/basic/

- Shizuoka Guide, Shizuoka Prefectural Tourism Association, 2009. http://www.fujisan223.com/en/

- Yamanashi Travel Guide, Prefecture Tourist Association, 2009. http://yamanashi-kankou.jp/english/index.html

ABOUT THE AUTHOR

Author (Richard Reay)

Richard first came to Japan as an exchange student while studying at the University of Lethbridge in Canada. He was so amazed by the friendly people and unique culture that he immediately returned after graduation. Since then Richard has lived in Hokkaido, Miyagi-ken and Niigata-ken before landing in Tokyo. Richard holds a Bachelor of Arts in Economics and a Master's Degree in Business obtained in Japan.

In 2008, he began working as a professional Mt. Fuji mountain guide. As one of the few non-Japanese official guides on Mt. Fuji he has been privileged to guide guests from all over the world, trek all four-summit routes and complete countless one-day, two-day, night and numerous pilgrim climbs from the base. He appeared on Japan's National Broadcasting Channel (NHK) in a show titled, Japan's 100 Most Famous Mountains as a professional Mt. Fuji guide. When not climbing Mt. Fuji, Richard teaches Economics at Asia University in Tokyo and owns and operates My Tokyo Guide Inc., a travel company based in Tokyo. My Tokyo Guide arranges a variety of custom and package tours, including Mt. Fuji climbing tours. For more information on My Tokyo Guide tours and packages refer to the following links.

MY TOKYO GUIDE INC.
MyTokyoGuide.com

Mt. Fuji Summit in May (Author)

INDEX

Index